Top 25 locator map ◄

GW00601205

TwinPack
Algarve

CHRISTOPHER CATLING

Christopher Catling has written more than 40 travel guides. He is a regular contributor to travel magazines on the Internet and in print. His books on London, Florence, Venice and Amsterdam are inspired by a keen interest in art and architecture, while his love of the countryside is reflected in guides to Madeira, Umbria and Crete.

If you have any comments or suggestions for this guide you can contact the editor at *Twinpacks@theAA.com*

AA Publishing

Find out more about AA Publishing and the wide range of travel publications and services the AA provides by visiting our website at *www.theAA.com/bookshop*

Contents

life *5–12*

how to organise your time *13–22*

top 25 sights *23–48*

About this book

KEY TO SYMBOLS

✚ Grid reference to the Top 25 locator map

✉ Address

☎ Telephone number

🕐 Opening times

🍴 Restaurant or café on premises or near by

Ⓜ Nearest underground (tube) station

🚉 Nearest railway station

🚌 Nearest bus route

⛴ Nearest riverboat or ferry stop

♿ Facilities for visitors with disabilities

✋ Admission charge

↔ Other nearby places of interest

❓ Tours, lectures or special events

▶ Indicates the page where you will find a fuller description

ℹ Tourist information

TwinPack Algarve is divided into six sections to cover the six most important aspects of your visit to the Algarve. It includes:

- The author's view of the region and its people
- Suggested walks and excursions
- The Top 25 Sights to visit
- The best of the rest – aspects of the region that make it special
- Detailed listings of restaurants, hotels, shops and nightlife
- Practical information

In addition, easy-to-read side panels provide fascinating extra facts and snippets, highlights of places to visit and invaluable practical advice.

CROSS-REFERENCES
To help you make the most of your visit, cross-references, indicated by ▶, show you where to find additional information about a place or subject.

MAPS
The fold-out map in the wallet at the back of the book is a large-scale map of the Algarve.
The Top 25 locator maps found on the inside front and back covers of the book itself are for quick reference. They show the Top 25 Sights, described on pages 24–48, which are clearly plotted by number (**1**–**25**, not page number) in alphabetical order.

PRICES
Where appropriate, an indication of the cost of an establishment is given by € signs: €€€ denotes higher prices, €€ denotes average prices, while € denotes lower charges.

ALGARVE
life

A Personal View

INTEGRATION

The Algarvian readiness to embrace all comers is part of a tradition of tolerance dating back many centuries. Many of the Jews expelled from Spain in 1492 by the Catholic monarchs Ferdinand and Isabella found a new home in the Algarve, and the region's architecture, cooking, ceramics and agriculture all result from the absorption of North African and Spanish settlers and their cultural influences.

Typical fishing vessel on the beach at Ilha de Armona

Building facades in Tavira

In the 1970s the Algarve like the rest of Portugal was just opening its doors to the world, having shrugged off a dictatorship that had come to power in 1932. The rest of Europe was also experiencing something of a revolution, the birth of mass tourism. It looked at the Algarve and fell in love with this tiny southwestern corner of Europe, finding its warm climate, fantastic beaches and welcoming people irresistible. It was a match made in heaven.

Thirty years on and the bond is stronger than ever, but the Algarve has matured from the shy debutante into the 'femme fatale', one of the

prime sunshine destinations in the Med and a year-round playground for all ages. Without doubt there have been changes. A traveller from those early pioneering days might lament the loss of prime coastal scenery to sometimes, dour apartment blocks and hectares of concrete. However, the Algarve hasn't been turned into a bland artificial 'holidayland'. One of its chief attractions in the early 21st century is it's multidimensional allure. It pleases the most diverse of tastes and it does it very well.

The coast, of course, is the lure for the vast majority of visitors and the Algarve offers a wealth of choice from long fine strands to bijou rocky coves. The sheltered eastern shore is perfect for bronzing while the more windswept west acts as a magnet for beachcombers and windsurfers. The Algarve's resorts are all anchored by excellent beaches – some such as Albufeira and Carvoeiro still support a fishing fleet of diminutive craft

The bell tower of Faro Cathedral

EXPORTS

Portugal is the world's biggest producer of cork, and much of it is grown in the Algarve and the Alentejo. Traditional almond and fig production, while still important, is in decline, but citrus production is increasing and large areas of the foothills are covered in orange and lemon groves. Tuna, cod and sardine fishing and canning are important, but the industry has not modernised and faces strong competition from Spanish fishermen with more modern fleets.

that set out each night in search of a fresh catch. Adults come to pit themselves against some of the best golf courses in the world, while children can spend hours splashing around at several enormous water parks.

Travel inland from the coast and the Algarve presents a different face. The hilly hinterland is dotted with whitewashed villages and swathed in forests of cork oak or cultivated with abundant citrus groves whose glorious scent hangs in the spring air. Exploration is delightfully untroubled either by car or on the numerous footpaths that weave beneath the trees. History's dusty hand has left a long legacy here – from Stone Age settlements to Roman villas and Moorish castles to Manueline chapels – perfect for those who want to touch the past. By contrast, exceptional modern developments such as the exclusive resort of Val do Lobo are sure to develop into tomorrow's architectural classics.

The lovely beach on the Ilha de Tavira

As the sun sets, the main resorts don a mantle of neon signs advertising some of the hottest nightlife in Europe. You can eat at a Michelin-starred restaurant, club till the early hours or try your luck at the casino. If this doesn't take your fancy, then spend the evening with the locals at a simple waterfront restaurant enjoying a plate of delicious grilled sardines washed down with fresh *vinho verde* wine.

Algarve in Figures

GEOGRAPHY

- The Algarve, Portugal's southernmost province, is separated from the Alentejo, the next province north, by a range of low mountains known as the Serra de Monchique to the west and the Serra do Caldeirão to the east.
- To the west and south the region is bounded by the Atlantic Ocean, and to the east the River Guadiana forms the frontier between Portugal and Andalucia (Spain).
- The Algarve represents about one-twentieth of Portugal's total area (4,960sq km) and measures about 135km east to west and between 27 and 50km north to south.

LANDSCAPE

- Topographically, the Algarve divides into three main regions: the coast (*litoral*), where most of the intensive tourist development is located; the foothills (*barrocal*), where most of the agriculture is concentrated; and the almost uninhabited mountains (*serra*), which support extensive cork oak forests.
- The Algarve includes mainland Europe's southwesternmost point, the legendary Cabo de São Vicente (Cape St Vincent). The western end of the coast is composed of eroded sandstone cliffs of many colourful hues, with numerous marine grottoes and wind-eroded rock stacks, while towards the east the coast is flat and sandy, with long beaches and barrier islands forming shallow lagoons.

CLIMATE

- The mountains separating the Algarve from the Alentejo also shelter it from cold continental air in winter, so that the region's winter climate is markedly milder than the rest of Portugal, though it does have high rainfall, due to Atlantic fronts.
- The coast is traditionally divided into the *barlavento* (windward) region (from Cape St Vincent to Albufeira), which bears the brunt of the southwesterly winds, and the more sheltered *sotavento* (leeward).

People of the Algarve

Henry the Navigator

Prince Henry the Navigator (Dom Henrique O Navegador, 1394– 1460) was the third son of João I of Portugal. Though he only ever made one sea journey, he nevertheless single-handedly set Portugal on the course that was to make her one of the great maritime powers of Europe. He did this by setting up a college at Sagres, symbolically choosing a point that looks out from the tip of Europe to what was then the vast unknown of the Atlantic. Gathering around him the best astronomers, naval engineers and navigators of his day, he funded their research and their voyages of discovery. The invention of the caravel, a small, light but extremely buoyant and manoeuvrable ship, eventually enabled explorers and merchants to reach India, the Far East and the Americas.

Gil Eanes

Theorising about the possibility of land beyond the horizon is one thing, but sailing into the unknown is a different matter, and Gil Eanes (c1400–88), a native of Lagos, was the brave navigator who took up the challenge. Sailing round the coast of West Africa in 1434, he led modern Europe's first-ever expedition around Cape Bojador, popularly believed to mark the end of the world, with only boiling monster-ridden seas beyond. Proving otherwise, Eanes mapped the coastal waters and encouraged others to follow in his wake.

Bartolomeu Dias

In 1487, Bartolomeu Dias (c1450–1500) set out from Portimão at the head of the first expedition since ancient Roman times to round the tip of southern Africa. The storm-battered tip, which he named Cape Torment because of its extraordinarily unpredictable currents, was more optimistically renamed the Cape of Good Hope on the instructions of King João II, who saw it as the route to the riches of the East. The Cape was to prove Dias' nemesis, for he died when his ship was wrecked sailing round it in 1500.

Statue of Henry the Navigator at Lagos

A Chronology

2000 BC	Bronze Age people migrate to the region from North Africa.
1000 BC	Phoenician traders from the eastern Mediterranean establish trading posts along the Algarve coast.
550 BC	The Carthaginians, from modern-day Tunisia, found the town of Portimão.
197 BC	The Romans invade the Iberian Peninsula and settle the Algarve. Resistance leads to years of guerilla warfare until Caesar quells the region in his campaigns of 61–45 BC.
5th century AD	Christianised Visigoths migrate into the Algarve from the north and settle in the region, establishing the first cathedral at Faro.
AD 711	Arabs invade the Algarve from Ceuta in Northern Africa and conquer the region.
AD 712	Moorish leader Muce-Ben-Noçair adopts Silves as the regional capital. The Moors name their new territory Al-Gharb, 'land of the west', from which the modern name, Algarve, is derived.
1189	The Christian Reconquest of the Iberian Peninsula achieves a notable victory at Silves, when the besieged city surrenders to an army led by King Sancho I.
1191	The Moors recapture the city and continue to rule in the Algarve, long after they are driven out of Lisbon and the north of Portugal.
1249	Sancho's successors, Afonso II and III, continue the struggle against the Moors, taking Tavira in 1239, then Faro and Silves. The Moors finally leave and the region becomes part of Portugal.
1443	Prince Henry the Navigator sets up his court at Sagres and establishes a school of navigation, ship-building and astronomy. He lays the foundation for Portugal's subsequent pre-eminence as a maritime trading nation.

1444 One of Europe's first slave markets is established at Lagos, following western exploration of what is now the Senegal estuary.

1485 Portugal becomes a major commercial power, with trading posts in western and southern Africa, Asia, Indonesia and Brazil. Lisbon is the departure point for voyages of discovery.

1580 The Algarve comes under Spanish rule after Philip II conquers Portugal.

1640 Border towns on the Guadiana River bear the brunt of the fighting as the Portuguese revolt against Spanish rule and regain their independence under King João IV.

1755 A series of earthquakes destroys many towns in the Algarve, and the subsequent tidal waves block river estuaries and ports with sand. The Marquês de Pombal, King José I's chief minister, rebuilds the region's towns.

1807 Napoleon invades Portugal and the royal family flees to Brazil. The Algarve puts up fierce resistance to the French. A group of fishermen from Olhão later sail to Rio de Janeiro in a tiny boat to tell their exiled king of Napoleon's defeat.

1932 President Salazar establishes a military dictatorship in Portugal. Portugal remains neutral during World War II, but severs relations with Nazi Germany.

1974 The Carnation Revolution: Portugal becomes a democracy after soldiers overthrow the postwar dictatorship.

1986 Portugal becomes a member of the EU.

2002 Portugal says goodbye to the escudo, as the euro is introduced.

2004 The new Algarve Stadium in Faro plays host to first round matches as Portugal hosts the European Football Championship.

Best of the Algarve

If you only have a short time to visit the Algarve, or would like to get a complete picture of the region, here are the essentials:

• Blow the cobwebs away on top of the cliffs at Fim do Mundo (World's End), as Cape St Vincent is known, gazing out over the waves to the distant horizon.

• Step back in time on a visit to Silves, which under Moorish rule boasted marble-clad palaces and bazaars full of eastern splendour.

• Leave the busy coastal resorts and head inland to explore rural Algarvian life. Either under your own steam or by jeep safari.

• Eat sardines for lunch. Unloaded fresh each morning they are charcoal-grilled at restaurants all along the coast, advertising their presence with a delicious scent.

• Walk to the Fonte de Benémola for a taste of the Algarvian countryside, as a contrast to the more developed coast.

• Visit Praia da Rocha at sunset to enjoy the changing colours of the sandstone rocks and cliffs as the sun goes down.

• Play golf at one of the Algarve's 24 golf courses, one of Europe's top golfing-holiday destinations.

• Join in a village festivity for the fun of noisy fireworks and to taste local wines and kebabs or fish cooked over an open wood fire.

• Spend a lazy day on the beach but rather than joining the hordes, head for one of the barrier islands, such as the Ilha da Tavira, and find your own private area of sand dunes and sea.

• Visit the capital, Faro, for its sophistication, timeless Old Town, ethnographic museum illustrating a way of life that only just survives, and to enjoy the frisson of the Capela dos Ossos (► 53).

Sample grilled sardines in Portimão

ALGARVE
how to organise your time

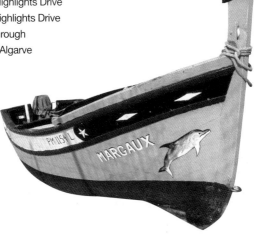

A Walk from Lagos to Luz

Early evening is a good time for this walk, when you can enjoy the sun set. Ambitious walkers can take the whole route from Lagos to Luz and back; alternatively you can take the bus one way and walk back – check the times of buses between Lagos and Luz at the tourist information centre. A third option, which is ideal for walkers with children, is to take the much shorter route to Ponta da Piedade and back.

INFORMATION

Distance 6km (1km from Praia do Camilo to Ponta da Piedade)
Time 3 hours (long walk); 30 minutes (short walk)
Start point Municipal tourist information centre in Lagos, or the Praia do Camilo car park
End point Luz
Lunch O Poço (€€)
    ✉ Avenida dos Pescadores, Luz
    ☎ 282 789189

Start from the centre of Lagos by walking west along the Avenida dos Descobrimentos, past the Forte da Ponta da Bandeira. Following the main road uphill and out of town turn left at the first set of traffic lights to Praia de Dona Ana.

Explore the beach at Praia de Dona Ana where the rocks are like fossilised sponge, then climb back up retracing your steps to the main road (300m), taking a left and continuing up the hill. After 500m you'll see a sign pointing left for Praia do Camilo. Leave the road and walk to the café at the cliff top where you can pick up the route (keep the sea on your left) for Ponte de Piedade. If you have a car leave it here by the café. Goats and walkers have eroded a number of tracks at this point but they all lead in one direction. Don't stray close to the cliff edge as rock falls and subsidence are not uncommon.

Walkers head out via a network of tracks, to the atalaia (obelisk) at the top of the hill above Luz

At Ponta da Piedade, you will find fishermen waiting to take visitors on short trips to the nearby grottoes.

From Ponta da Piedade, the path turns westward and follows the cliff-tops. Porto de Mós, with its beach and café, is reached after about 20 minutes. From here, a track continues westwards, levelling out on the cliff-tops, and continuing for some 50 minutes to Luz.

The most prominent feature in the landscape is the *atalaia* (obelisk) above Luz, which marks the highest point (109m) reached by the cliffs on this stretch of coast.

A Walk from Monchique to Caldas de Monchique

This gentle stroll takes you through the attractively wooded countryside surrounding Monchique to the pretty spa town of Caldas de Monchique (► 30).

Start in Monchique's main square, Largo dos Chorões. Head south on the main N266 Portimão road.

During spring, you will enjoy the almond-like scent from the mimosa trees that line the roads around Monchique.

After 10 minutes, you will reach the junction between the main Portimão road and the Alferce road, which goes off to the left (east). Take the narrow road between the BP petrol station and the restaurant.

The road now follows the right bank of one of the many small streams that spring up in the Serra da Monchique, eventually flowing down to the sea at Portimão. The road descends through olive groves and orange plantations. To the left you may catch sight of Picota, the Algarve's second highest peak (774m).

After 25 minutes or so, you will cross the Marmelete road. Cross to the continuation of the road on the opposite side. Where it forks, after five minutes, stay on the road, which bears left. Continue downhill to Caldas de Monchique – the track runs parallel and eventually joins the N266 road on the edge of the town.

As you approach Caldas, look out for the strawberry trees that grow abundantly in the humid environment of the spa town. The fruits of these low-growing evergreen trees are used to produce a fermented liquor which is distilled to make *medronho*. Reward yourself with a glass on completing the walk, but beware – the deceptively smooth taste disguises an alcoholic kick that can be up to 90 per cent proof.

INFORMATION

Distance 4km
Time 1½ hours
Start point Tourist Information centre, Largo dos Choroes, Monchique
End point Caldas de Monchique
Lunch 1692 (€€€)
✉ Caldas de Monchique
☎ 282 910910

Take a break on a shady terrace in Caldas de Monchique

15

A Walk through the Salt Pans of Castro Marim

INFORMATION

Distance 8km

Time 3 hours

Start/end point At the Town Cemetery

Lunch Restaurant Páo Quente (€)
✉ Rua de Sáo Bartolomeu Sul, Castro Marim
☎ 281 513033

The castle walls in Castro Marim look down on acres of salt pans, many of them in use since pre-Roman times. Now protected as a nature reserve, these salt pans, and the tidal creeks that run through them, are home to many species of bird. Take binoculars with you.

Park by the town cemetery on the south-western outskirts of town. Walking away from the main road (keeping the cemetery wall on your right), follow the raised path that threads through the reserve, with the main channel of the fish-filled creek to your left.

On your right, the flower-filled fields are planted with olive trees, where storks nest. These huge birds may flap lazily overhead from time to time. Also visible are egrets, dipping their beaks in the silt at the edge of the salt pans in search of food, and the occasional shy flamingo. If you tire of the heat (there are no trees and no shade on this walk) you can retrace your steps. Alternatively, you can follow the path all the way round the reserve. At its westernmost point it passes the still-working salt pans at Aroucas, where salt obtained by evaporation is piled up in a great pyramidal heap.

From here the path turns southwards, almost to the suburbs of Monte Gordo, visible (but not accessible) across the Carrasqueira estuary. The path follows the northern bank of the estuary, over several footbridges, before rejoining the outward path: turn to the right to return to the car park.

A view of the flat salt pans of the Reserva do Sapal nature reserve in Castro Marim

Eastern Highlights Drive

Explore the empty hills of the Serra do Caldeirão, with their abandoned windmills and scattered cork oaks, then follow the scenic Guadiana River.

From Tavira, head north on the N397 for 33km to Cachopo. The countryside consists largely of shallow, acidic schistic soils that are not very fertile, though cork oaks thrive. In between the forests are hills covered in wild cistus and holly oak. Cachopo produces sheep's milk cheese and sweet, air-cured mountain hams.

Continue north on the N124 for 16km to Martinlongo, then south on the N506 for 12km to Vaqueiros. Just north of Vaqueiros, visit the Cova dos Mouros mine, which was worked from the Copper Age (3500 BC) onward; it is now an industrial museum (► 56).

Drive a short distance south, then turn left (east), signposted Melhedes/Soudes and continue for 18km to the junction with the N122; head left (north) for 13km to the junction with the N124, then right (east) on the N124 for 6km to Alcoutim. Stop for lunch in Alcoutim (► 26), then explore the castle.

Head south on the road that follows the River Guadiana. In Guerreiros do Rio, stop to visit the former school, which now houses a small river museum. Farther on, as you enter Montinho das Laranjeiras, look out for the roman ruins lying by the roadside immediately before the bridge; the remains consist of a villa and an early Christian church, with apse and stone-lined graves.

When the river road meets the N122, turn left (south) and continue for 8km to Azinhal, noted for its lacework. Approaching Castro Marim (► 31), there are views to the left of the suspension bridge carrying the IP1 motorway across the River Guadiana to Seville, in southern Andalucia. To return quickly to Tavira, join the motorway here and head west.

INFORMATION

Distance 160km
Time 1 day
Start/end point Tavira
Lunch O Soeiro (€)
    ✉ Rua do Município 4, Alcoutim
    ☎ 281 546241

The red-tiled rooftops of Alcoutim stand in stark contrast to the whitewashed buildings

17

Central Highlights Drive

This drive takes in farming hamlets, green river valleys, gnarled olive trees and scented orange groves. Consider stopping for a leisurely lunch in Alte or Querença.

From Loulé, head out west on the N270 road signposted to Boliqueime. As you leave the town, a wide new road to the left leads up to the unusual modern church of Nossa Senhora da Piedade. It is worth driving up for the views from the terrace in front of the church and for the little 16th-century chapel alongside.

Continue to Boliqueime and take the road north (signed Lisbon) to Paderne (➤ 39).

Take the road north out of the town and divert left to explore the well-preserved 12th-century castle above the River Quarteira.

Drive on through the village of Purgatório, continue to Portela de Messines, then turn right for Alte. Alte (➤ 28) is the Algarve's most attractive village. The church was built in the 13th century by the local overlord as a thank-offering for his safe return from the Crusades, and has some fine statuary and tile work.

The river tumbles through the village, over a mini waterfall and past converted mill buildings. Continue eastwards, stopping to scale Rocha da Pena, if time allows, or to explore Salir castle (➤ 55).

From Salir take the minor road south to Vicentes, and turn left. After 2km, the road crosses a bridge, turns sharp left in front of a mill, and then sharp right. Continue on to Querença, then to the main road and turn right to return to Loulé.

INFORMATION

Distance 74km
Time 7 hours
Start/end point Loulé
Lunch Fonte Pequenã
bar/restaurant (€€).
Located at the *fontes*
(springs), signposted
approximately 400m
from the the town.
☎ 289 478509

Fonte Grande Springs in Alte

A Drive through Central Algarve

This splendid half-day drive takes in the historic town of Silves and the mountain scenery of the Serra de Monchique, but it can be extended to a whole day.

From Portimão, cross the River Arade using the old bridge and follow the minor road to Lagoa. Church lovers will want to stop in Estômbar for the Manueline portal and *azulejos*, and in Lagoa for the São José Monastery, with its pretty cloister.

From Lagoa, head north on the N124 to Silves, passing under the new motorway. Approaching Silves from the south gives a fine view of the walled hilltown and its castle. Park by the river and climb up to the castle, cathedral and archaeological museum (▶ 57).

Leave Silves on the road to São Bartolomeu de Messines, stopping to look at the Cruz de Portugal beside the roundabout as you exit the town's suburbs. After 5km, turn left for a view of the Barragem de Arade reservoir. Follow the minor road that leads, via Amorosa, to São Bartolomeu, and join the IP1 (also signposted the N264/E01) to Lisbon. Leave at the next exit, after 15km, signposted to São Marcos da Serra and Nave Redonda. Cross the railway line west of the IP1 to find signs to Monchique.

Many distractions may tempt you to stop – you could take a closer look at the cork oak trees to see how the bark is stripped, or perhaps enjoy the wayside wild flowers. At Nave Redonda, in the Alentejo, turn south to return to the Algarve along a scenic road that climbs to Monchique (▶ 37).

You can extend the tour by climbing Fóia, the Algarve's highest peak (▶ 37), or choose a restaurant and enjoy lunch with views.

Head south to Caldas de Monchique (▶ 30) and stroll around the flower-filled streets. To return to Portimão, continue south on the N266.

INFORMATION

Distance 110km
Time 6 hours
Start/end point Portimão
Lunch Paraíso da Montanha
(€€)
✉ Estrada da Fóia, Monchique
☎ 282 912150

The thick, rust-coloured curtain walls of Silves Castle

19

Finding Peace & Quiet

WALKING

The Algarve Walkers Club is a group of English expatriates living in the Algarve who meet for weekly rambles.
☎ 282 698676 for further information.

The salt pans in Tavira at dusk

Sealife flourishes in the sheltered lagoons of the Ria Formosa Natural Reserve

AWAY FROM IT ALL

The Algarve is at its most developed south of the IP1 motorway between Faro and Albufeira. Simply to drive away from this area is to escape quickly and easily from the bustle of modern life and discover the many faces of the Algarve. South of Faro is the extensive Reserva Natural da Ria Formosa (➤ 43), a series of salt-water lagoons and salt pans separated from the open sea by scores of sandy islands, some tiny, others stretching for several kilometres. The warm lagoon water supports many types of marine life. This in turn attracts flocks of wading birds, from shy flamingos to the storks that flap lazily over the roof-tops, building their nests on church towers, telegraph poles and ancient olive trees.

Farther west, the marsh systems and river estuaries around Portimão, Lagos and Burgau are full of birds. You do not have to be a knowledgeable ornithologist to spot the ubiquitous flocks of cattle egrets, with their hunched shoulders, long probing beaks and pure white feathers, or to enjoy the hunting skill of the kestrels and sparrowhawks that skim the fields in search of prey.

BIRD MIGRATION

The Algarve is an important staging post for migrating birds, which pass down through the Iberian Peninsula in October before making the final leg of their journey to Africa. Returning the same way in March and April, they ride the southwesterly winds from Africa, exploiting the fact that spring and summer come early here in order to feed on the insects that are already thick in the air before heading for nesting sites in northern Europe. Cape St Vincent, Europe's southwesterly tip, is the place to see birds streaming past the cliffs or using the updraughts to carry them inland – these range from large seabirds, such as gannets, skuas, petrels and shearwaters, to swallows, swifts, warblers and colourful bee-eaters.

The spectacular Algarvian countryside is a paradise for walking enthusiasts

INLAND ALGARVE

The hilly Algarvian interior is covered in a network of paths and mule tracks, which are perfect for exploring on foot. Large-scale walking maps are difficult to come by and generally out of date, but the Algarve Tourist Authority publishes a *Guide to Walks*, containing 20 short routes, and more ambitious walks are detailed in the excellent *Landscapes of Portugal*, by Brian and Eileen Anderson (Sunflower Guides).

Walkers head for the Algarve any time from late October onwards, but the best time to come is March to May, when the countryside is a mass of flowers and butterflies. A short walk in the hills will take you from orange groves, heady with the cloying scent of citrus blossom, to bare slopes dense with sticky-leaved cistus (rock rose), bearing big white flowers. Rarer flowers bloom in the undergrowth, including many varieties of orchid, as well as numerous bulbs, such as the petticoat-hoop narcissus. Every wayside is bright with the searing yellow of the Bermuda buttercup, which colonises every inch of uncultivated space, and the sound of cicadas in the undergrowth can reach a deafening pitch.

Delicate blossom of an almond tree thrives in the fertile sun-drenched countryside of the Algarve

21

What's On

FEBRUARY
Carnival (weekend preceding Shrove Tuesday): steel barriers seal off town centres from traffic. Typically, Saturday sees local children in a costume parade, while the irreverent 'satirical parade' takes place the following day. Loulé Carnival has the biggest and best procession. Be warned that water bombs, eggs, flour and other substances can be hurled at spectators during carnival parades, so don't wear your best clothes.

APRIL
Holy Week (especially Palm Sunday, Good Friday and Easter Saturday): religious processions in the streets of many towns, when actors re-enact scenes from the Passion and Crucifixion of Christ.

MAY
May Day Folk Festival (1 May): traditional singing and folk dancing, with food and drink on sale in Alcoutim, Albufeira, Alte and Monchique.

MAY/JUNE
International Music Festival: sponsored by the Gulbenkian Foundation, this is the biggest arts festival in the Algarve, with top international artists performing in a number of centres, including Albufeira and Silves.

JULY
Algarve Jazz Festival (all month): local and international musicians.
Alcoutim Handicraft Festival (2nd or 3rd week): the best of the region's crafts.
Silves Beer Festival (all month): Silves Castle is taken over by brass bands and folk dancers.
Feira do Camo: Faro's own handicraft festival.

AUGUST
Fatacil (3rd week): Lagoa's country fair is a showcase for local agriculture, industry and commerce. Music and food and wine tastings.
Summer in Tavira: *fado*, folk and classical music, plus folk dancing in the city's parks and gardens.
Fish Festival (11 Aug): Cabanas celebrates with a market, folk music, dancing and *fado* music.
Banho de 29 (29 Aug): fireworks and live music to celebrate the end of the holiday season in Lagos.

SEPTEMBER
National Folklore Festival (1st week): Portuguese folk music and dancing troupes from as far away as Brazil and Madeira.
Lagoa Wine Festival (2nd week): tastings to promote local vintages.
Nossa Senhora das Dores (3rd week): country fair food stalls, fairground attractions and folk concerts, starting in Monte Gordo and moving on to Tavira.

ALGARVE'S
top 25 sights

The sights are shown on the maps on the inside front cover and inside back cover, numbered **1**–**25** alphabetically

Albufeira

INFORMATION

✚ B3
✉ 36km west of Faro
🍴 Cafés (€) in Rue 5 de
   Outubro; O Penedo (€€)
   in Rua Latino Coelho 15
🚌 Buses from Faro
ℹ️ Rue 5 de Outubro
   ☎ 289 585279
↔️ Loulé (➤ 35)

The narrow cobbled streets of this old fishing village now play host to boutiques, bars and restaurants.

Albufeira typifies the way that tourism has transformed the sleepy fishing towns of the Algarvian coast into today's bustling holiday resorts. Until the 1960s, only fishermen used the beach below the town. They still do, bringing in their daily catch every morning, but now they are surrounded by thousands of sun-bronzed bodies.

The narrow cobbled streets of the old town now play host to boutiques, bars and restaurants, and the beach is reached by a tunnel. The streets are paved with black and white mosaics, a traditional form of paving that was originally invented as a way of using up the rubble from houses demolished by the 1755 earthquake.

However, Albufeira has grown so big that it takes in many adjacent bays, and a more modern centre of tourism has grown up 2km to the east centred on 'The Strip', a street of English style pubs, bars and restaurants at Montechoro. To the west of the old town an impressive modern marina with multi-coloured buildings adds a new glamour to the established resort.

The coastline around Albufeira has several good bays where the beaches have attracted hotel development, including Praia du Gale, 8km west, which has excellent watersports.

Above: *The narrow cobbled streets of the old town*

Right: *Albufeira's Old Town Beach*

Algar Seco (Carvoeiro)

If you want to laze around on a beach, Algar Seco is an excellent choice with its colourful cliffs and rock stacks.

There is a marked difference between the beaches of the sandy eastern *sotavento* (leeward) section of the Algarve and the rocky western, or *barlavento* (windward) section. Armação de Pêra, to the west of Albufeira, is the axis on which the Algarve is tilted and the point at which this decisive change takes place. West of here the land rises gradually until it reaches the high cliffs and boiling seas of Cape St Vincent; to the east, flatter coastal terrain gives way to endless strands of golden sand, gently dipping into a warm and shallow sea.

The cause of the tilt is the collision zone between the Eurasian and African continental plates, which lies only a short way south of the Algarvian coast. The African plate is moving northwestwards, pushing the European land mass slowly upwards. This explains why the junction between land and sea is more dramatic in the west, marked by steep sandstone cliffs, and why the coast is broken up into a series of rock-strewn coves.

The result is a series of wind-and-sea eroded rocks whose evocative shapes make this part of the coast unique, and nowhere else has these rock formations in such quantity or variety as Algar Seco. Here, children will love exploring the rock platforms and pillars, the arches, chambers and caves, the miniature gorges, clefts and pools that litter the shore. Snorkellers will find weed-encrusted rocks like miniature coral reefs below the waves. There is not much sand, but the other features compensate, including the colourful show of light and shade that begins as the sun sinks at dusk.

INFORMATION

➕ B2

✉ About 1km east of Carvoeiro, signposted to the left from the centre of town

🍴 Small café (€) among the rocks; several others in Carvoeiro (▶ 50)

♿ Free

Algar Seco Rock formation

25

Alcoutim

INFORMATION

➕ D1
✉ 40km north of Vila Real
de Santo António
🍴 O Soeiro café (€ ➤ 68)
↔ Castro Marim (➤ 31)
ℹ Rua 1st de Maio
☎ 281 546179

*Above: The remains of
the castle walls at
Alcoutim*

*Below: The castle ruins;
a reminder of the days
when Alcoutim was
originally a fortified
stronghold and strategic
river port*

**Alcoutim has the atmosphere of a
timeless town. Life moves at the pace
of the horse-drawn ploughs that are
still used to till the surrounding fields.**

Ferrymen frequent the O Soeiro café, just above
the quay, and take passengers across the river to
San Lúcar in Spain on request. There are no
border controls, so it is easy to slip across the river.

Both towns are dominated by their castle.
Sanlúcar's is the biggest – a massive structure
crowning the cone-shaped hill above the town –
but Alcoutim's is the oldest. The excavated
remains of Roman structures have been overlaid
by 11th-century Moorish remains, in turn
superseded by a 1304 fortress. Both castles are a
reminder of former hostilities between Spain
and Portugal.

Besides Alcoutim's castle, the other good
viewpoint in town is the Ermida de Nossa
Senhora da Conceiço (Hermitage of Our Lady
of Conception). This whitewashed church,
approached via an 18th-century stone staircase,
stands at the highest point in the village and
allows intimate views down into the village
gardens and across the flat rooftops of the
simple, cube-shaped houses.

Almancil

Almancil boasts some of the best interior design galleries, shops and restaurants along the Algarve as well as a delightful church.

Almancil has little traditional character but has grown rapidly in recent years, becoming a service centre for the upmarket resorts at Vale do Lobo and Quinta do Lago.

One outstanding attraction draws visitors here – the church of São Lourenço dos Matos (St Lawrence of the Woods), beside the main N125 road east of the town (just before the start of the Almancil bypass). The interior of this domed, whitewashed church is covered in blue and white *azulejos*, dating from 1730. The side walls have six scenes from the saint's life. The gilded altarpiece, typical of those found on the Algarve, is known as *talha dourada*. Just below the church, the Centro Cultural São Lourenço displays modern art and hosts jazz and contemporary music concerts.

INFORMATION

+ C3
- 13km northwest of Faro
- Church open daily 9–1 and 2:30–6
- Café (€) in Centro Cultural
- Moderate

Centro Cultural São Lourenço
- 289 395475
- Tue–Sun 10–7

Above: *The whitewashed, domed exterior of the church of San Lorenzo*

Above: *Sculpture in São Lourenço Cultural centre*
Left: *Beautiful azulejos decorate the white-washed walls of the church of São Lourenço*

27

Alte

INFORMATION

➕ C2

✉ 20km north of Albufeira

🕐 Church: daily 8–1, 3–7

🍴 Fonte Pequeña bar/
restaurant (€€)
☎ 289 478509

♿ Free

↔ Loulé (➤ 35),
Silves (➤ 45)

Above: *The restaurant on
Fonte Grande Springs*

*Water cascades from the
Fonte Grande Springs in
Alte,*

Discover the many charms of this pretty hill village, built around a series of gushing springs (fontes).

Alte sits on top of a hill in the limestone foothills known as the Barrocal. Winding roads climb to the village through a region dubbed the 'Garden of the Algarve', where fig trees and citrus groves surrounded by drystone walls alternate with almond orchards and stands of gnarled and ancient olive trees.

The focal point of the village is the parish church, one of the most interesting in the Algarve because of its wealth of 18th-century woodwork and its baroque *azulejos*. Rope mouldings (in the Manueline style) decorate the west door, the vaulting of the chancel and the arch of the so-called 'Chapel of the Landowner', with its coat of arms of the counts of Alte. Painted and gilded woodwork surrounds the altar, while angelic musicians and cherubs scamper among the vine and acanthus leaves.

From the church, cobbled lanes lead eastwards for a short stroll to a series of springs *(fontes)*, where the water gushes out of pipes set in niches decorated with *azulejos* and plaques inscribed with verses by the local poet, Cândido Guerreiro (1871–1953), in praise of water. The water here betrays its volcanic origins with a sulphur smell, but it tastes fresh enough and many local people believe that the water prolongs their life and keeps them healthy.

About 200m upstream is another set of springs, Fonte Grande. From here, keen walkers can follow the footpath upstream for 3km to the source of the River Alte in the foot of the Serra do Caldeirão mountain range. Less keen hikers can rest at one of the two restaurants, or picnic at tables under the shade of the trees, before browsing through the crafts on sale in the *artesanato* shops around the church square.

Cabo de São Vicente

Come at sunset on a clear day to get the most from the cliffs that were once believed to mark the end of the world.

Cabo de São Vicente is the most southwesterly point of the European mainland (not counting Madeira, the Canary Islands and the Azores). It really looks and feels like the end of the earth (which is why centuries ago the Portuguese dubbed it 'Fim do Mundo'). With its towering cliffs plunging 70m to the pounding surf, and its stiff westerly breezes, this is a place that stirs the imagination and works a strong magic over the many visitors who flock here.

The Romans, recognising the spiritual pull of the spot, built a temple to the presiding *numen* (deity). Nothing now remains of this, but there is a lighthouse whose beam can be seen up to 100km out to sea. The lighthouse is open to visitors if the keeper is not otherwise engaged. If you do get to look inside, you will see Europe's biggest lighthouse lantern, lit by a massive 3,000-watt bulb.

Your own memories and impressions will be dictated by the weather: stallholders selling chunky handknitted sweaters in the car park are a reminder that it can be chilly here no matter how hot it is a few miles inland, and there can be fog, rain or howling gales. On the other hand, nothing enhances the pristine beauty of Cabo de São Vicente more than watching sea birds playing in the air above the crashing waves, or the sight of the rose-tinted sun sinking slowly into the ocean at dusk.

INFORMATION

- A3
- 6km west of Sagres
- Snack bars on site and cafés (€) in Sagres
- None
- Free
- Sagres (➤ 44)

Above: *White foam laps the shores of Cabo de São Vicente*
Below: *The Cabo de Sao Vicente lighthouse*

Caldas de Monchique

INFORMATION

🔲 B2
✉ 20km north of Portimão
🏠 1692 (€€€)
☎ 282 910910
🚌 Bus service links Caldas de Monchique to Portimão
♿ None
💳 Free
❓ For more information: www.monchiquetermas. com is the spa website

Above: *The gardens and fine buildings of the tiny spa town of Caldas de Monchique*

Below: *The delightful fountain in the centre of Monchique, the source of the commercially bottled water*

Visit this centuries–old spa town in the Monchique hills and sample the sulphurous waters once enjoyed by the Romans.

Caldas de Monchique is a charming little spa struggling to maintain its position long after has it ceased to be the fashionable resort of bourgeois Portuguese looking for an instant cure-all. These days people come as much to enjoy the typically Algarvian food in many of the local restaurants as to put themselves through the strict dietary regime normally involved in a spa cure.

As with many spas built at the crux of the 19th and 20th centuries, the buildings reflect the belief that good company and relaxation are just as important for the cure as water consumption – hence a casino was regarded as *de rigueur* and the hotels were built with grand public rooms for dancing and conversation. The spa complex has benefited greatly from a recent renovation project and was reopened with great aplomb by the Portuguese Minister of Tourism in the summer of 2001.

The Romans got here first. More than 2,000 years ago they built a spa on the site of the present sanatorium, calling it Mons Cicus, from which the spa, and the nearby market town of Monchique, derive their name. Today it is the picturesque appearance of the little spa that appeals, set amongst dense woodland on the edge of a mini ravine, with its pastel-painted houses in fanciful styles.

Footpaths thread through woods and along the river, taking you to springs where you can sample the water – pleasant enough to taste even if it is warm and smells sulphurous. For something stronger, there are cafés where you can sip coffee, or try the local speciality medronho, a fiery liqueur distilled from fermented arbutus berries.

Castro Marim

At Castro Marim there are two huge castles to explore, spreading across the two hills that rise above the salt flats either side of this fishing town.

The main castle, to the north of the town, was built in 1319 as the headquarters of the crusading Order of the Knights of Christ, founded in 1119 as the Knights Templar. The knights played a decisive role in the Christian Reconquest of Portugal. The older medieval castle is now entirely contained within the walls of its 17th-century successor, which is six times larger.

A rampart walk allows you to stroll all the way round the castle, with views down to the fishermen's houses, built with flat roofs for drying fish. Within the castle walls are the offices of the Castro Marim Nature Reserve.

The São Sebastião fortress, on the opposite hill, dates from the 17th century and is part of a much bigger complex of defensive walls that survive only in parts around the town. Like its medieval counterpart, the fortress served as a base from where to defend the entrance to the River Guadiana, bearing the brunt of hostilities between Portugal and Spain. Today, the two countries have abolished their common border and the modern suspension bridge, which crosses the river, carries the IP1 motorway, 2km northeast of the town.

INFORMATION

- D2
- 4km north of Vila Real de Santo António
- Cafés (€) in Rua de São Sebastião
- Buses from Vila Real de Santo António
- 2-4 Rua José Alves Moreira
  ☎ 281 531232

Castelo and São Sebastião fortress
- Apr–Oct 9–7; Nov–Mar 9–5. Closed public hols
- Free

Above: *A view from the flat salt pans of the Reserva do Sapal nature reserve in Castro Marim*

One of two commanding castles that dominate the town of Castro Marim

Cova dos Mouros Parque Mineiro

INFORMATION

🔲 D1

✉ 10km southeast of
   Martinlongo, 2km south
   of Vaqueiros

☎ 289 498505

🍴 Café on site

⏲ Apr–Oct daily 10:30–6;
   Nov–Mar Tue–Sun
   10:30–5. Closed 18 Dec to
   20 Jan

♿ Few

💷 Expensive

↔ Cachopo (➤ 17)

This museum has been created around the spoil tips and shafts of an abandoned copper mine.

The open-air mining park at Cova dos Mouros is well signposted as you drive south along the N506 road from Martinlongo to Vaqueiros. Located in the empty, scrub-covered hills of the northern Algarve the mine has been in use for more than 5,000 years. The workings were rediscovered in 1865 and have only recently been developed into this unusual attraction – now designated an ecological park.

The park centres on the reconstruction of a Chalcolithic village (2,500 BC), which re-creates the lifestyle of the very first miners. Staff, dressed in animal skins, work the ground with copies of ancient tools.

After you have learned about the mining activities, Cova dos Mouros offers other ways to spend a pleasant few hours. The park is one of several across Spain and Portugal that works for the survival of the Iberian donkey. Once so numerous as beasts of burden, these gentle, hardy creatures have now almost disappeared throughout the peninsula. Children will enjoy the rides they give across the surrounding countryside.

If you prefer to walk, there are posted routes where you can take in the upland flora and fauna. In spring copious wild flowers, including rare orchids, blanket the ground, and even in the height of summer butterflies and lizards provide interest as you stroll. Finally, you can enjoy a cooling dip in the natural pools of the Foupana River and you may catch a glimpse of a family of otters.

Part of the mining heritage at the Parque Mineiro, Cova Dos Mouros

Estói

Decades of neglect have only added to the charm and appeal of the palace garden in Estói.

Behind high walls, in the little village of Estói, lies a lavish rococo palace, built in the 18th century for the Conde de Carvalhal. The family wealth declined, and the palace was acquired by Faro city council some years ago, the plan being to restore the building for use as a *pousada* (state-run luxury hotel). The building remains empty and much of the grounds are off limits but the main entranceway from the church square leads down a cobbled road to the heart of the complex for wonderful views of the outer façade and tantalising glimpses across the faded grandeur of the formal garden, with its palm-lined avenues and terraces.

Designed to please the senses, the walls of the garden are decorated with *azulejos* depicting bucolic scenes of shepherds and shepherdesses, while naked youths frolic with dolphins in the fountains. Elsewhere, buxom goddesses drape themselves langorously around water-filled shells, against a tiled background of cranes and bullrushes. On the lower terrace, a stone-lined nymphaeum shelters a copy of Canova's famous statue *The Three Graces*, flanked by ornate mosaics.

Climb the ornate stairway to the upper entrance courtyard from where you'll get the best views of the palace itself, the soft pink hue of the walls deepens as the sun drops and there are innumerable decorative details to admire. Regular visitors would probably prefer Estói to be kept this way, as they have come to love the softened outlines of crumbling balustrades, the crooked steps and loose cobbles, and the ghostly atmosphere.

INFORMATION

✚ C3

✉ Rua da Barroca, Estói

☎ 289 997282

🕐 Tue–Sat 9–12:30, 2–5:30. Closed Sun, Mon and public hols

🍴 Sol Algarvio (€) and Ossonoba (€) opposite the church

♿ Few

🎫 Free

🔄 Vila Romana de Milreu (► 36)

❓ Plans to restore the palace for use as a *pousada* are due to commence 2005; therefore it might not be possible to view

Above: *Fine sculptures scattered about the grounds of the Palacio de Estói*

Tilework that adorns the terraces of Palacio de Estói

Lagos

INFORMATION

➕ A2

🚉 Lagos railway station
   ☎ 282 762987, 1km
   north of the town centre

🚌 Bus terminus: Rossio de
   São João
   ☎ 282 762944, with
   services to and from
   Aljezur, Burgau,
   Odeceixe, Portimão,
   Sagres, Salema and Vila
   do Bispo

↔ Luz (► 51)

ℹ Rue Vasco da Gama,
   São João
   ☎ 282 763031

*The statue of King
Sebastian in Lagos*

Lagos is an atmospheric town encircled by massive 16th-century walls that effectively shut out the 21st century.

The walls shield Lagos from western Algarve's biggest concentration of hotel developments to the west of the town. Holidaymakers tire of the beach and drift into Lagos to discover a maze of cobbled streets, too narrow for cars to penetrate. Café owners have set up tables and chairs, tempting visitors to stop and sample their delicious coffee and cakes, in between exploring the town's churches, museums, art galleries, antique shops and bustling market.

Parking spaces are available along the Avenida dos Descobrimentos, the palm-lined road that runs alongside the River Bensafrim. Sheltered from the open sea, the river was adapted for use as a canal to provide access to the town's harbour. Sleek white yachts and battered fishing boats sit side by side in the modern harbour, and signs point the way to the offices of companies offering fishing trips and voyages to the caves and coves of Ponta da Piedade (► 40).

The social hub of Lagos lies at Praça Gil Eanes, with a huge statue of Dom Sebastião at the centre of the square. This modern statue (1973), the work of sculptor João Cutileiro, portrays Prince Sebastian, who believed it was his mission to conquer North Africa and convert the Moors to Christianity. He gathered an army of 18,000 men and set sail from Lagos in 1578. When his ill-equipped army met a vastly superior force at Alcacer-Quibir, in Morocco, only 100 Portuguese survivors emerged from the battle to tell the tale.

Loulé

Loulé is a city to savour at leisure, from the early market to attractive streets and historic buildings.

The second most populous city in the Algarve combines bustling modernity – symbolised by the space-age church prominently sited on the hilltop to the west of the city – with narrow, cobbled alleys in the old town around Largo de São Francisco. From here, pedestrianised Rua de 5 Outubro leads to Largo Dr Bernardo Lopes, at the foot of Praça da República, the city's main street. The first right turn takes you to Loulé Museum of Archaeology (▶ 56).

Opposite (on the corner with Rua Vice-Almirante Cândido dos Reis) is the delightful Espírito Santo monastery, with its quiet, shady cloister. Part of the monastery has been turned into a Municipal Art Gallery, with changing exhibitions by contemporary artists. Heading downhill, cobbled Rua das Bicas Velhas ('The Street of the Old Spouts') is named after the spring-fed drinking fountains, set below a coat of arms, at the bottom of the street.

To the right of here, Praça Dom Alfonso III takes you outside the ancient city walls for a view back up to the surviving medieval towers. Loulé's parish church, São Clemente (▶ 53), dominates the large town square. To the west of the church is the palm-shaded Jardim dos Amuados, the enigmatically named 'Sulky People's Garden'. In the opposite direction, Rua Martim Farto leads to the Municipal Market, a vast Moorish-style building that covers a whole block in the city centre. Both within the market and in the surrounding streets are shops and stalls selling just about everything.

From the colourful market, with its façade decorated with art nouveau tiles, Praça da República runs downhill, back to Rua 5 de Outubro, lined with many cafés.

INFORMATION

🔲 C2

🚌 Bus terminal is in Rua Nossa Senhora de Fátima
☎ 289 416655, with services to and from Albufeira, Almancil, Alte, Armação de Pêra, Faro, Lagoa, Messines, Portimão and Quarteira

🔄 Alte (▶ 26)

🔰 Edifício do Castelo, Rua de Paio Peres Correia 17
☎ 289 463900

Museu Arqueológico

✉ Rua de Paio Peres Correia 17
☎ 289 400624
🕐 Mon–Fri 9–5:30, Sat 10–2
♿ Few
🎟 Cheap

São Clemente

✉ Largo Batalão dos Sapadores do Caminho
🕐 Daily 10–1, 2–7
♿ Few
🎟 Free

Pirr Pirr pepper, Loulé Municipal Market

Milreu

INFORMATION

➕ C2

✉ On the western outskirts of Estói, well signposted from main approach roads

☎ 289 997823

🕐 Tue–Sun 9:30–12:30, 2–6 (until 5 Oct–Apr) Closed Mon and public hols

🍴 Cafés (€) in front of parish church

♿ Few

💶 Moderate

↔ Palácio de Estói (➤ 33)

ℹ Junta de Freguesia
   ☎ 289 991620

Exploring the extensive remains of the Roman villa at Milreu demonstrates how little life in the Algarve has changed.

At Milreu, you will discover that wealthy Romans enjoyed houses that are not so different, in many respects, from today's luxurious holiday homes.

The villa was probably built by a 1st-century AD fish magnate – perhaps the owner of a fish-processing factory, where locally caught sardines, tuna and swordfish were dried and salted before being packed in barrels for export. This theory is based on the fact that the wonderful mosaics that decorate many of the rooms show fish leaping in and out of the frothy waves. These denizens of the deep adorn the walls and rooms on both sides of the villa – the bathhouse to the left (west), with its hot and cold pools and its hypocaust system for providing underfloor heating, and the living quarters, to the right (east). Separating the two is a large courtyard garden which was once surrounded by a shady pillared colonnade.

Another plausible theory is that this was not a private villa at all, but a spa and temple complex. The huge building that survives to roof height to the east of the site is interpreted as a nymphaeum, a shrine to the local water nymphs, which was converted for use as a church in the early Christian period, reusing the pools and piscinas as baptismal fonts. Visitors coming to worship at this shrine would have used the bath facilities, which are somewhat grand for just a private villa. The sheer number of stone cubicles in the *apodyterium* (changing room) alongside the bath complex would seem to support the theory that this was a public facility. The modern museum foyer offers an interesting contrast to the ancient remains beyond.

Monchique

Monchique attracts summer visitors seeking an escape from the roasting sun of the coastal resorts and to walk in the mountains.

The main town in the Serra da Monchique mountain range is located 458m above sea level and the tree-shaded town usually feels several degrees cooler. Monchique has many natural springs, and the nearby spa village of Caldas de Monchique (▶ 30) is the source of the commercially bottled water sold all over the Algarve. Springs feed the fountain that adorns Monchique's main square, Largo dos Chorões. Cafés, craft shops and art galleries ring the square, offering free tastings of *medronho*, produced by distilling the fermented fruits of the strawberry tree (summer only).

Ornate 16th-century carvings decorate the parish church, Nossa Senhora da Conceição, and the gilded altar has many charming details, including angels holding up the sun and the moon. In one of the side chapels, look out for the *azulejos* depicting St Michael in combat with the devil, and the suffering souls in Purgatory.

Many visitors go on to enjoy lunch in one of several restaurants lining the Fóia road that specialise in chilli-flavoured chicken *piri-piri.* You can work up an appetite first by walking to Fóia, the Algarve's highest peak, or following the signposted footpath above the town hall that leads to the ruins of Nossa Senhora do Desterro monastery, a short stroll with fine views.

INFORMATION

- B2
- 24km north of Portimão
- Cafés in Monchique (€), restaurants on the Monchique to Fóia road
- Buses from Portimão and Silves
- Portimão (▶ 41)
- Largo dos Chorões
  ☎ 282 911189

37

Olhão

INFORMATION

➕ C3
✉ 8km east of Faro
🍴 Cafés (€) near the market
🚌 Bus station on Avenida
General Humberto
Delgado
☎ 289 702157.
Buses to Cacela, Faro,
Fuzeta, Moncarapacho,
Monte Gordo, Tavira, Vila
Real de Santo António
ℹ Largo Sebastiāno Martins
Mestre 8A
☎ 289 713936

Museu da Cidade
✉ Edifício do Compromisso
Marítimo
🕐 289 700184

Olhão is, along with Portimão, the biggest of the Algarve's fishing ports and although it has been modernised it has lost none of its character.

The eastern end of the town is dominated by warehouses and canning factories. The fish market along the seafront, with its patterned brick walls and corner turrets, has been altered to meet EU health regulations, but has retained its vitality. Equally colourful is the fruit and vegetable market, its stalls piled high with dried figs, almonds, honey, herbs and local cheeses, as well as fresh fruits.

On the opposite side of the seafront promenade Olhão has some of the Algarve's most attractive and ornate buildings, with curvaceous balconies, decorated with wrought-iron flowers and acorn finials. One fine group of buildings lines the same square that houses the tourist information centre, one block from the seafront, and there are more in the streets radiating north – look above the shop façades in the main commercial streets to take in the detail.

A maze of cobbled pedestrian-only streets leads to the town's main church, Igreja Matriz, with its marvellously theatrical baroque façade. Inside, life-size angels flank the splendid, gilded altar. Behind the church, the newly opened Museu da Cidade holds temporary exhibitions and there is a small gallery displaying prehistoric and Roman finds.

Slices of pumpkin for sale at Olhao at the Saturday market

Paderne

Paderne is an attractive village and a retreat for wealthy Algarvians who have built high-walled villas and cultivated beautiful gardens.

For visitors, it is not the village that is of interest so much as the castle on its outskirts. The castle is well signposted from Paderne. You can either drive all the way, or walk the last two kilometres.

Drive through the village northwards (downhill), and turn left at the right-angled bend at the bottom of the main street. As you exit the town, look for another left turn (signposted *'Fontes'*). The track leads to a commercial water bottling plant, where spring water gushes from spouts into a large, stone trough.

Turn left at the plant, then immediately right and follow the red earth track that winds through fields. At the next junction, turn left and follow the track up to the castle.

If you would rather walk the last stretch, turn right at the junction and continue until the track ends by the river. Park and enjoy the view across the Ribeira de Quarteira to the water mill on the other side. At this point a track leads straight on along the river bank. If you walk along it for 1km, you will reach a 16th-century packhorse bridge with its grinding stones lying among the weed-covered walls. Beside the bridge, a steep path climbs up to the right and leads, after another 1km, to Paderne Castle.

The castle's external walls survive to a good height, but it is not possible to explore the interior of the castle. Rubble fills the chapel that was built after the castle was conquered in 1249 in a fierce and bloody battle between the Moors and the Christian army of King Afonso III.

The ambience of the site is somewhat spoilt by traffic noise, but you'll have panoramic views of the countryside.

INFORMATION

➕ C2
✉ 12km north of Albufeira
🕐 Castle open 24 hours
🍴 Cafés (€) near the parish church
🔁 Loulé (➤ 35)

Ponta da Piedade

INFORMATION

🔼 A3

✉ 2km south of Lagos

🍴 Bar Sol Nascante (€), opposite the lighthouse

🚢 Bom Dia Actividades Marítimas

   ✉ Marina de Lagos

   ☎ 282 764670

   🕐 Office: 9–6 in winter; 9–9 in summer. Closed Jan and Feb. Cruises: daily, plus sunset cruises in summer departing 7:30PM

💶 Free

↔ Historic centre and museums of Lagos (➤ 34)

Consider taking a trip by boat to explore the spectacular free–standing pillars, rock stacks and grottoes of this cove near Lagos.

For coastal scenery, the coves around Ponta da Piedade are hard to beat. The same geological processes and erosive forces that carved out the rock sculptures at Algar Seco (➤ 25) have been at work here too, creating a coastline of ochre and rust-red cliffs, stacks and arches, which resemble the ruins of some fantasy castle.

From the cliff-tops at Ponta da Piedade you can walk along a path to the various sea grottoes, but the going can be precarious. From the lighthouse at Ponta da Piedade, for example, there are paths ranging all along the coastline with views to the foaming waters below, but vertigo sufferers may find it a problem. There is also a set of steps descending the cliff face from the lighthouse down to a rock platform where local fishermen wait to take passengers on short coastal trips to see the cliffs between here and Praia da Luz. This is well worth doing, especially during the nesting season, when you may get a good close-up of cliff-nesting birds, such as the heron-like cattle egrets and little egrets.

Coastal scenary of Ponta da Piedade where cliff erosion has left an array of free-standing pillars, stacks, arches and caves

Another option is to join one of the boat trips that depart regularly from Lagos, such as those operated by Bom Dia. Trips usually last from 10 until 2, or from 2:30 to 6, but full-day trips are available as well, allowing time for swimming, snorkelling and lunch on board ship.

Portimão

Portimão is one of the Algarve's main fishing ports, and there is much local life to be enjoyed in and around the city's harbour.

Portimão is one settlement where tourism hasn't yet stamped its indelible mark. There is much local life as the catches are brought in at the city's harbour where a long landscaped waterfront promenade allows for easy strolling.

Fishing trips, for beginners and experienced anglers, Arade River cruises to Silves and trips to explore the caves and cliffs at Algar Seco (▶ 25) are advertised around the quay. The tantalising smell of grilled sardines rises above numerous atmospheric eateries just off the quayside (enter through a short tunnel under Rua Serpa Pinto) housed in the humble houses where the fisherman used to live.

Portimão, with its high-quality shops, is also an excellent place to visit if you prefer real shops to those geared to tourists. Heading inland from the harbour, Rua Dr João Vitorino, Largo 1 de Dezembro and Rua Direita offer plenty of choice. Largo 1 de Dezembro is laid out as a park, with fountains and flower beds, and the benches are decorated with *azulejo* pictures depicting key events in Portuguese history. The pictures date from 1924, when Portimão was granted city status by the Portuguese president, Manuel Teixeira Gomes, a native of the town. The adjacent town hall is a fine 18th-century palace, once home to the viscounts of Bívar. The largest church in the Algarve, the Jesuit Igrejo do Colegio, is on the Praça da República.

The 1920s were a prosperous time for Portimão and many of the buildings lining the centre were given decorative tilework façades and pretty wrought-iron balconies, reflecting the art nouveau designs that were then in vogue.

INFORMATION

- B2
- 18km east of Lagos
- Cafés and restaurants (€) along the quayside
- Railway station 1km to the northwest of the city centre, on Largo Sarrea Prado
- Bus station on Largo do Dique
  ☎ 282 418120.
  Buses to Albufeira, Alvor, Armação da Pêra, Faro, Ferragudo, Lagoa, Lagos, Loulé, Monchique, Praia da Rocha, Silves and Torralta
- Avenida Zeca Afonso
  ☎ 282 416556

41

Praia da Rocha

INFORMATION

➕ B2
✉ 2km south of Portimão
🍴 Café in the Forteleza (€)
🚌 Buses from Portimão
↔ Carvoeiro (➤ 50)

Rock formations at Praia da Rocha

One of the most photographed places in the Algarve, this is also one of the regions most hedonistic resorts.

Praia da Rocha's distinctive, ochre-coloured sandstone columns rise from a broad south-facing beach and attract amateur and professional photographers alike. The resort is also popular with young visitors dedicated to making the most of the famed nightlife on Avenida Tomás Cabreira, the disco- and bar-lined seafront road backed by high-rise hotels. At the eastern end of the 2km beach, the Fortaleza de Santa Catarina looks across to Ferragudo's Castelo de São João de Arade. The two fortresses form a 17th-century defensive system designed to guard the Arade River estuary. If you are seeking an escape from the crowds, take a boat trip to the rocky coves at Praia da Vau and Praia dos Três Irmãos.

Reserva da Ria Formosa

Learn all about the wildlife of the Algarve's lagoons, and meet an unusual breed of poodle.

The Ria Formosa Nature Reserve stretches for some 30km along the coast, from Anção, west of Faro, to Manta Rota, near the Spanish border. It consists of scores of sandy islands, linked by shallow lagoons, salt marshes and water channels, which are home to birds, plants and insects. While the outer islands facing the Atlantic bear the brunt of oceanic wind and waves, these shallow lagoons are warm and sheltered, providing perfect spawning conditions for many fish, and an ideal feeding ground for birds.

The best place for getting acquainted with the complex ecology of the reserve is at the visitor centre at Quinta do Marim, 1km east of Olhão. Displays provide information on conservation activities and wildlife, and maps can be obtained showing recommended walking routes. You can also enquire about visiting the kennels where the rare Portuguese water dog, the Cão de Água, is bred to save it from extinction. These endearing 'poodles', with big limbs and curly black hair, have web-like membranes between their paws which enable them to swim very effectively. Algarvian fishermen once trained the dogs to help them by diving and shepherding fish into their nets.

Two areas of the reserve are readily accessible by boat: ferries depart from the harbour in Olhão to the Ilha da Armona (daily at 8:30, 12 and 5; last boat back at 5:30), and to Farol, on the Ilha da Culatra (daily 11, 3 and 6:30; last boat back at 7:15). From these sand spits you can watch the bird life of the lagoons, or find your own private strip of unspoilt beach and sand dune for sunbathing. It is also one of the best places along the coast for a picnic accompanied by a bottle of Portuguese wine.

INFORMATION

➕ C3

✉ Visitor centre: 1km east of Olhão, signposted to the Parque Natural, and *campismo* (campsite)

🕐 Visitor centre: Mon–Fri 9–12:30, 2–5:30. Closed Sat, Sun and public hols

🍴 Small café at the visitor centre; plenty of choice in Olhão (€–€€)

↔ Olhão (➤ 38)

43

Sagres

There are many cliff-top walks here and in spring and autumn you can watch migrating birds flying over the headland or wheeling past the cliffs.

Sagres is Europe's most southwesterly community. Just 6km east of Cabo de São Vicente (► 29), it sits atop a rocky plateau, scoured by the same winds that send the sea crashing against the rocks of the nearby beaches. Even more bleak is the promontory south of the town, the site of the Fortaleza (Fortress) de Sagres, where Prince Henry the Navigator established his school of seamanship in 1443.

The sailors who came to study here lived an almost monastic life as they prepared to sail to new worlds, having mastered astronomy, navigation and cartography. The walls of the small town that Henry had built on the cliff-tops still survive, offering superb views across the rocky promontory, as does the simple chapel, with its altarpiece (currently under renovation) depicting St Vincent holding a ship. Near by is a 15th-century Rosa dos Ventos (wind rose) inscribed into the rock, 43m in diameter, which may once have been fitted with a weather vane to indicate the wind direction. The Vila do Infante, where Prince Henry lived, along with many other original buildings, was destroyed by the English buccaneer Sir Francis Drake in 1587, when Portugal was under Spanish rule.

Although the modern town has little to hold the attention, there are compensations to living in Sagres, including pristine coves to explore. Local fishermen keep the restaurants well supplied with fresh fish and seafood, and also offer boat trips to view the magnificent Costa Vicentina from the sea. There are many cliff-top walks, and in spring and autumn you can watch migrating birds flying over the headland or wheeling past the cliffs.

A rugged cliff rising out of the ocean on the peninsula of Sagres

Silves

The former Moorish town of Xelb is overlooked by the Algarve's best-preserved castle, the massive Castle of the Moors.

This compact town is built on terraces between the River Arade and the massive castle. One way to approach the town is by sailing from Portimão along the route taken by Phoenician traders who established their base here in the 1st millennium BC. Their riverside colony became the Roman city of Silbis, and then, from the 8th century, the Moorish city of Xelb. Described by Arabic chroniclers as ten times more impressive than Lisbon, Xelb was a city of gleaming domes and minarets, of poets, writers and musicians, traders, craftsmen and farmers.

Due to the earthquake of 1755, little now survives of the Arabic influence – at least in architectural terms. The most lasting legacy is visible in the almond and citrus groves that you see from the castle walls across the surrounding countryside; the Moors introduced these crops, along with the irrigation system.

The castle was built to last and, despite bearing the brunt of fighting during the Christian Reconquest in the 12th and 13th centuries, it is substantially intact. Excavations are uncovering its secrets: exposed walls show the remains of Phoenician and Roman fortifications and the Moorish rulers' palace.

From the castle, narrow cobbled streets descend steeply to the cathedral (➤ 53) and the archaeological museum (➤ 57). From the museum it is a short stroll through the Torreão das Portas da Cidade, the medieval town gate, to the the Praça do Municipio, with its town hall, ancient pillory and pavement cafés. Shop-lined streets lead from here to the covered market and the embankments of the River Arade and its pavement cafés.

INFORMATION

➕ B2
🚉 Railway station 2km south of town
🚌 Bus terminus alongside Mercado Municipal
☎ 282 442338, with sevices to and from Albufeira, Armação de Pêra, Lagoa, Messines, Monchique and Portimão
🚹 Rua 25 e Abril
☎ 282 442255
↔ Portimão (➤ 41)

The dignified lofty aisles of Se de Santa Maria, one of the few remaining Gothic monuments in the Algarve

45

Tavira

INFORMATION

✚ D2

🚉 Railway station is on Rua da Liberdade

🚌 Bus terminus is in Rua dos Pelames
☎ 281 322546, with services to and from Cabanas, Cacela, Faro, Monte Gordo, Olhão, Pedras d'El Rei, Santa Luzia and Vila Real de Santo António

↔ Olhão (➤ 38)

ℹ Rua da Galeria
☎ 281 322511

Castelo

✉ Calçada de Paio Peres Correia

🕐 Daily 9–5:30

🎫 Free

♿ Few

View of Tavira

Wealth from the Portuguese colonies was lavished on Tavira's numerous churches, whose turrets and belfries add interest to the skyline.

This distinctive town has a greater variety of architectural detail than most. Both banks of the River Gilão, which passes through the centre, are lined by noble houses with baroque window frames and balustraded parapets. Most have wrought-iron balconies, whose decoration is mirrored in the railings of the pedestrian bridge that links the two sides of the town. The hip-gabled roofs are highly distinctive, known as *tesouro* (treasure) roofs.

The best place to view all Tavira's architectural diversity is from the walls of the Moorish castle on the south bank of the river. The castle was rebuilt after the Christian Reconquest and the present walls date from the reign of Kinf Dinis (1261–1325). Cross the footbridge, take the first turn right, climbing uphill, past the tourist office, and pause to admire the superb Renaissance doorcase to the Church of Nossa Senhora da Misericórdia (Our Lady of Mercy). Above the portal, angels hold aside curtains to reveal the figure of the praying Virgin. Turning left takes you to the castle, and to the hilltop church of Santa Maria do Castelo.

Heading north from the castle, turn down Rua Detraz dos Muros to Rua dos Pelames; this riverside street has some rare 16th-century houses, distinguished by stone doorcases which survived the 1755 earthquake. Crossing the footbridge again takes you down Rua 5 de Outubro to São Paulo church. Restaurants and bars line the square in front of the church (Praça Dr Padinha), and the streets running to the south and east. Look out for the latticed doors, made of turned and woven strips of wood.

Vilamoura

The purpose-built resort of Vilamoura has, at its heart, a large marina ringed by shops, bars and restaurants, but the site has surprising history.

From here it is a short walk to the sandy beach, and there are further beaches near by at Falésia. The region benefits from excellent golf courses, tennis centres, fitness centres, horse-riding schools and watersports facilities, all within walking distance. Though the current resort dates back only to the 1970s, the site has an interesting history. The Cerro da Vila Museu e Estação Arqueológica, north of the waterfront, is a new archaeological park created at the site of a Roman settlement and later Moorish farm. Remains include the floor plan of a Roman villa, complete with bathhouse.

INFORMATION

- C3
- 11km southwest of Loulé
- Restaurants (€–€€€) around the marina
- From Faro and Quarteira

Cerro da Vila
- Avenida Cerro da Vila
- 289 312153
- 9:30–12:30, 2–6
- Moderate

A traditional-style, modern apartment development near Vilamoura

47

Vila Real de Santo António

INFORMATION

- 🔲 D2
- ✉ At the eastern edge of the Algarve, 23km east of Tavira
- 🍴 Cafés (€) in Praça Marquês de Pombal and pedestrian streets north of the square
- 🚌 Bus station on Avenida Casal Ribeiro (☎ 281 511807) with services to and from Altura, Cacela, Castro Marim, Faro, Manta Rota, Monte Gordo, Olhão and Tavira
- ↔ Castro Marim (➤ 31)

Ayamonte

- ✉ In Spain, on opposite bank of River Guadiana to Vila Real
- 🍴 Cafés (€) and restaurants (€) in Plaza de la Ligna

Museu Manuel Cabanas

- ✉ Rua Dr Teófilo Braga 38
- 🕐 May–Sep daily 4–midnight; Oct–Apr Mon–Fri 10–1, 3–7
- 🎫 Free

Built in just five months in the late 18th century, Vila Real has remained in a time warp in contrast to the Spanish city of Ayamonte across the river.

Vila Real was founded by Royal Charter in 1773 and represents the town planning ideals of the Marquês de Pombal (1699–1782), Portugal's chief minister under King José I (1714–77). It was the Marquês who planned this city to represent the rational ideals of the Enlightenment, in contrast to the Spanish city of Ayamonte on the opposite bank of the River Guadiana.

Ayamonte has prospered, as shown by its gleaming white tower blocks and modern port facilities, while charming Vila Real is locked in time. Vila Real's riverside embankment is lined by grand hotels and scores of restaurants and shops catering for the Spanish bargain hunters who come here to buy household goods, tempted by low prices.

One block inland from the river embankment, the legacy of the Marquês de Pombal is evident in the strict grid of streets and the geometrical precision of the elegant main square, Praça Marquês de Pombal, with its church, town hall and former infantry barracks. In the centre of the square, the obelisk monument to King José I acts like the needle of a giant sundial, casting its shadow on the traditional black and white mosaic paving.

In 1991, a new suspension bridge opened across the River Guadiana, linking Portugal to Spain, but the river ferry continues to do a brisk trade, plying the river at roughly half-hourly intervals, from 9 until 9. This is a good way of sampling the different cultures of the two countries (don't forget that Spain is usually an hour ahead of Portugal, and that almost everything shuts for the siesta during the afternoon, from 1 to 4).

ALGARVE'S
best

49

Beaches

ARMAÇÃO DE PÊRA

Armação de Pêra is a burgeoning resort full of multi-storey apartment blocks and hotels, sprawling along a broad stretch of sandy beach that marks the watershed between the rocky coves of the western Algarve and the sandy shores of the east. Visitors can laze on the sands within sight of the colourfully painted boats belonging to the local fishing fleet, or engage in the many activities on offer, such as surfing or snorkelling.

✉ 12km west of Albufeira 🍽 Santola Restaurante, Largo da Fortaleza
☎ 082 312332 🚌 Buses from Portimão and Albufeira 🔁 Albufeira
(➤ 24) 🚹 Avenida Marginal ☎ 282 312145

The coastline near Carvoeira

CABANAS

Cabanas is a low-key resort just to the east of Tavira. It has a broad, sandy beach facing a long sandbank, with a warm and shallow lagoon providing sheltered bathing conditions that attract families with children. A 5km-stroll along the beach leads to the fortified village of Cacela Velha, a tiny hamlet consisting of a church and a few cottages surrounded by massive walls.

✉ 5km east of Tavira 🍽 Café (€) in Cacela Velha 🚌 Buses from
Tavira 🔁 Tavira (➤ 46)

CARRAPATEIRA

Sleepy Carrapateira owes its popularity to its proximity to some of the west coast's best beaches. Amado, farther south, has the so-called Pedra do Cavaleiro (Knight's Rock) to protect it. The thundering surf all along the coast here appeals to watersports enthusiasts, but the landscape of towering cliffs and miles of sand is just as attractive for walkers and photographers.

✉ 35km northwest of Lagos 🍽 Small café (€) in main square
🚌 Bus from Lagos 🔁 Lagos (➤ 34)

Brightly painted fishing boats pulled up on the beach at Armação de Pera

CARVOEIRO

Carvoeiro is a pretty fishing village that remained virtually untouched until the 1980s. Ringed by Moorish-style buildings and the battlemented remains of former fortifications, the sheltered beach can get very crowded at the height of the season, but local fishermen will happily take visitors on trips to the other beaches, such as Benagil and Marinha, and to the nearby caves and rock stacks of Algar Seco (➤ 25).

✉ 16km east of Portimão 🍽 Cafés (€) and seafood restaurants (€€)
in Estrada do Farol 🚌 Buses from Portimão 🔁 Portimão (➤ 41)
🚹 Praia do Carvoeiro (☎ 282 357728)

ILHA DE TAVIRA

This 10km-long island, with its sandy beaches and sheltered bathing, is the most accessible of the barrier islands in the Ria Formosa Nature Reserve (➤ 43). Ferries make the short crossing from the Quatro Águas jetty, on the south bank of the River Gilão. You can also walk to the island across the footbridge from Santa Luzia, the seafront fishing village 3km west of Tavira.
✉ Just offshore from Tavira 🕒 Ferries run 8AM–11PM, May–Oct
🍴 Cafés (€) at northeastern tip of island 🎟 Free

LUZ

Recent developments have been handled with less care but Luz is still an excellent base for family holidays. The sheltered beach at Praia de Luz has rock pools to explore as well as decent sandy stretches and at the height of the season there is a well-organised watersports school and sea sport centre offering tuition for sailing, diving and windsurfing. A number of artificial scoops from the beach rocks have been identified as ancient tanks for salting and curing fish. A gateway on the seafront promenade leads to the scant remains of a Roman villa. At the other end of the village is a 17th-century fortress, which has been turned into a popular restaurant.
✉ 8km west of Lagos 🍴 Numerous cafés, including the Kiwi (€) on Avenida do Pescadores; Fortaleza da Luz (€€) 🚌 Bus from Lagos
♿ Few 🔄 Lagos (➤ 34)

MONTE GORDO

Separated from the beach by a wide, café-lined avenue, the hotels of Monte Gordo look down on one of the Algarve's finest beaches – a vast, broad sweep of golden sand. Numerous seasonal seafood restaurants and cafés, housed in makeshift timber cabins, sit along the sands, offering fresh fish provided by the local fishermen. With its warm waters, gentle offshore breezes and endless sands, Monte Gordo is a popular place for novice windsurfers to take their first tentative lessons, and there are plenty of beachside businesses offering watersports equipment and tuition.

Ilha de Tavira beach, Tavira

✉ 5km southwest of Vila Real de Santo António 🍴 Cafés (€) along Avenida Infante Dom Henrique 🚌 Buses from Vila Real de Santo António ℹ Avenida Marginal ☎ 281 544495 🔄 Vila Real de Santo António (➤ 48)

SALEMA

Despite the shops, bars and restaurants, Salema still has the air of an unspoiled coastal village, where the fishermen haul in their catch by the first light of dawn. Several offer fishing excursions. Equally popular are birdwatching excursions into the marshes west of the village. There is a sheltered beach at Ponta de Almadena, and another at neighbouring Boca do Rio; the two are linked by a 2km cliff-top walk.
✉ 15km west of Lagos 🍴 Several cafés and bars (€) in Rua dos Pescadores 🚌 Bus from Lagos ♿ Few 🔄 Lagos (➤ 34)

51

Churches

IGREJA DO CARMO AND CAPELA DOS OSSOS, FARO

The Igreja do Carmo, built in 1719, has an imposing baroque façade, flanked by twin bell-towers. The main altar and the side altars are decorated in the typical Portuguese baroque style known as *talha dourada*, with extravagantly carved and gilded woodwork, featuring scores of cherubs playing amongst acanthus leaf and vine foliage. In 1808 it was here that the people of Faro met, under the pretence of holding a normal religious service, to plot their ultimately successful resistance to the Napoleonic occupation of the town.
✉ Largo do Carmo

Igreja do Carmo

IGREJA DE SANTA MARIA DO CASTELO, TAVIRA

Standing alongside the castle, Tavira's parish church incorporates the minaret of the town's Moorish mosque, remodelled to form the clock tower. Inside are the fine 13th-century tombs of seven knights of the crusading Order of St James, whose ambush and murder prompted the Christian Reconquest of the city. As well as fine tilework and gilded altar surrounds, the sacristy has a museum displaying vestments and chalices.
✉ Calçada de Paio Peres Correia ⏲ Apr–Oct daily 10–12:30, 2–6; Nov–Mar daily 2–6. Closed public hols ♿ Few 💲 Free

Igreja de Santa Maria do Castelo

Igreja de Santo António

IGREJA DE SANTO ANTÓNIO, LAGOS

St Anthony's is one of the most lavishly decorated churches in the Algarve. Early 18th-century carved and gilded woodwork covers the entire east wall and frames wall paintings, showing scenes from the life of St Anthony. Study the carving closely and you will find miniature scenes from everyday life.
✉ Rua General Alberto da Silveira ☎ Tue–Sun 9–12.30, 2–5.30. Closed Mon and public holidays 💲 Free

IGREJA DE SÃO LAURENÇO DOS MATOS, ALMANCIL

One outstanding attraction draws visitors to Almancil – the church of St Lawrence of the Woods, beside the main N125 road east of the town (just before the start of the Almancil bypass). The interior of this domed,

whitewashed church is covered in blue and white
azulejos, dating from 1730. The side walls have six
scenes from the saint's life. The gilded altarpiece,
typical of those found on the Algarve, is known as
talha dourada.

✉ 13km northwest of Faro ⏰ Church open daily 9–1 and 2:30–6
🍽 Café (€) in Centro Cultural ⭐ Moderate

IGREJA DE SÃO PAULO, TAVIRA

Entered through a classical portico, more like a Greek
temple than a church, St Paul's is unusual for the
heavy, dark woodwork of its two side altars, ornately
carved but not covered in gold. The fine collection of
religious statues includes a delicate 15th-century
Flemish Virgin.

✉ Praça 5 de Outubro ⏰ Apr–Oct daily 10–12:30, 2–5; Nov–Mar
daily 3–6. Closed public hols ♿ Few ⭐ Free

SÃO CLEMENTE, LOULÉ

The narrow alley opens out into the square that is
dominated by Loulé's Gothic parish church, São
Clemente. The tower survives from the 12th century,
originally built as the minaret, or prayer tower, of the
city's Moorish mosque. Though now hung with bells,
and given a short dome and steeple, the minaret is one
of the few examples of Arabic architecture to survive
in the Algarve. Inside are several splendid side chapels
– notably the 16th-century São Brás chapel and the
São Crispim chapel.

✉ Largo Batalão dos Sapadores do Caminho ⏰ Daily 10–1, 2–7
♿ Few ⭐ Free

SÉ (CATHEDRAL), SILVES

Built on the site of the Moorish mosque to symbolise
the expulsion of the Moors from the city, the
magnificent 13th- to 15th-century cathedral is one of
only a few in the Algarve to retain its medieval feel.
Free from the gilded baroque woodwork of many post-
earthquake churches, the rose-pink granite columns
and vaults soar above the tombs of medieval knights
and bishops.

✉ Rua da Sé ⏰ Daily 8.30–6.30 ♿ Few ⭐ Free

SÉ (CATHEDRAL), FARO

Faro's cathedral is a fine example of both change and
continuity, standing on the site of the main mosque of
the Moorish city, which itself replaced the remains of a
Visigothic church built on the ruins of the Roman
basilica. The 1755 earthquake demolished much of
the original 13th-century cathedral, leaving only the
truncated stump of the tower. The interior can be
deliciously cool on a hot summer day. The Gothic
chapel on the south side, with its rib vaults and bosses,
survives from the 15th century, and the rest is typically
18th century, with gorgeous gilded woodwork and blue
azulejos.

✉ Largo da Sé ⏰ Mon–Fri 10–12, 2–5. Closed Sat, Sun and public
hols ♿ Few ⭐ Moderate

CAPELA DOS OSSOS

Attached to the Igrejo do
Carmo, the Capela dos Ossos
is a must for unsqueamish
children, who will find this
ghoulish site enormous fun.
Unfortunately, the Carmelite
monks who created the
chapel from the bones of
their pre-deceased brothers
would be horrified at such
disrespect. Perhaps the
intended memento mori
effect (the inscription over
the entrance translates as
'Stop here and think of the
fate that will befall you')
would have been better
achieved by a less decorous
arrangement of skeletal
remains.

Towns and Villages

KING JOAO II

King João II died in Alvor in 1495. Dropsy was given as the official cause of his death, but many suspected that he was poisoned by Spaniards, intent on the conquest of Portugal.

Typical Algarvian houses in Alvor

ALJEZUR

Aljezur is the largest town on the scenic N120 road to Lisbon. High on the hill above the town are the ruins of the massive 10th-century Moorish castle, captured by Dom Paio Peres Correia in 1246. He is said to have charmed a beautiful Moorish maiden who opened the castle doors to him one moonlit night. Good beaches near by include Arrifana (10km southwest), and Amoreira/Monte Clérigo (8km northwest). Some 17km north is the pottery-producing village of Odeceixe.

🖂 30km northwest of Lagos 🍴 Café (€) in Largo 5 de Outubro 🚌 Irregular bus service from Lagos 🛈 Largo do Mercado Estrada Nacional (☎ 282 998229)

ALVOR

Alvor is on the eastern edge of the wide Baia de Lagos, a shallow, bird-filled lagoon formed by the estuary of four rivers. Fishing inspired the carvings that decorate the portal of the 16th-century parish church. Local fishermen join the wading birds in the tidal estuary, searching for razor shells and clams, which are sold in the fish market on the harbour, and which are the principal ingredient of the seafood dishes served locally. For a closer look at the lagoon, follow the raised footpath that winds between the salt pans close to the shore. A swathe of land east of the town has been commandeered by several large modern hotel complexes, with development reaching all the way to Praia de Alvor and Praia dos Três Irmãos and almost filling the gap between Alvor and Praia da Rocha. The hotels are well placed for days on the beach or the relative bustle of nearby Portimão and Lagos.

🖂 4km west of Portimão 🍴 Àbabuja (€€) 🚌 Bus from Portimão 🛈 51 Rua Dr Alfonso Costa (☎ 224 57540)

The turquoise blue waters of the coastal fishing village of Ferragudo

FERRAGUDO

Located on the opposite side of the Arade River estuary from Portimão, Ferragudo is a rare example of an almost untouched coastal fishing village, a reminder of the Algarve as it was less than two decades ago. A timeless atmosphere prevails in the narrow cobbled streets which lead uphill to the simple village church, from whose terrace there are sweeping views over the rooftops across the boat-filled estuary.

✉ 2km east of Portimão 🍴 Cafés (€) along the harbour front
🚌 Buses from Portimão and Albufeira

FARO

Visitors arriving at Faro airport could be forgiven for judging the Algarvian capital to be a dusty industrial town with nothing to offer. So it looks from the airport road, with its jumble of seemingly unplanned tower blocks and light-industrial estates. Yet, at the centre of all this chaos, there is a quiet walled city of immense historic character, as well as a lively shopping centre, where cosmopolitan Faroites meet for lunch in the outdoor cafés of the traffic-free streets, or stroll after work in the cool of the evening.

✉ 32km southeast of Albufeira 🚌 Bus terminus is in Avenida da Republica (☎ 289 899760) with buses services to and from most main towns 🛈 Rua da Misericórdia 8–11 (☎ 289 803604)

PORCHES

Porches is the centre of the Algarve's pottery industry. Though the village is small, there is plenty to see here, as you browse through displays of terracotta jars and watch artists painting plates and fruit bowls with sunflowers, cockerels or

Pottery urns outside a shop in Porches

colourful clusters of grapes. Be sure to check whether flower pots and urns are frost proof, otherwise they will shatter if left out over the winter in colder climates. A trip to Porches can be combined with a visit to the Big One theme park (▶ 58), between Porches and Alcantarilha.

✉ On the N125 highway, 16km east of Portimão 🍴 Cafés in main square or Porches Velho (€€) 🚌 Buses from Portimão and Albufeira

SALIR

Salir's huge 12th-century castle survives in the form of a cobbled rampart walk, which passes some huge bastions of concreted rubble, all that remains after villagers robbed the walls of their facing masonry in the past. From the western stretch of the ramparts, there is a good view over the hillside olive groves and the patchwork of cultivated fields in the valley below to the Rocha da Pena. The castle is one of the few Moorish structures to survive in the Algarve, and its scale is illustrated by the number of more recent houses that now fill the interior. Though heavily defended, the castle fell to Christian forces in 1249, towards the end of the campaign to drive the Moors from Portugal. The parish church occupies a high platform (shared with a huge water tower) with fine views over the Barrocal countryside.

✉ 14km north of Loulé 🍴 Café Moura (€), Rua dos Muros do Castelo

55

Museums

COVA DOS MOUROS PARQUE MINEIRO

Well signposted as you drive south along the N506 road from Martinlongo, this open-air Mining Park at Cova dos Mouros (► 32) centres on the reconstruction of a Chalcolithic village (2,500 BC). It re-creates the lifestyle of the very first miners, and staff dressed in animal skins work the ground with copies of ancient tools. This museum has been developed around the spoil tips and shafts of an abandoned copper mine that has been in use for more than 5,000 years. The workings were rediscovered in 1865 and have only recently been developed into this unusual attraction – now designated an ecological park.

✉ 10km southeast of Martinlongo, 2km south of Vaqueiros ☎ 289 498505 🍴 Café on site ⏰ Apr–Oct daily 10:30–6; Nov–Mar Tue–Sun 10:30–5. Closed 18 Dec to 20 Jan ♿ Few 💷 Expensive

FÁBRICA DO INGLÊS AND MUSEU DA CORTIÇA, SILVES

A cork factory near the river has been transformed into a leisure complex with gallery space, restaurants, street entertainment and a water show with lights and music. The complex features a Cork Museum, celebrating one of Portugal's most important exports.

✉ Rua Gregório Mascarenhas ☎ 282 440440; www.fabrica-do-ingles.com ⏰ Apr–Oct daily 9:30–12:45, 2–9:45; Nov–Mar daily 9:30–12:45, 2–6:15

MUSEU ARQUEOLÓGICO, FARO

Faro's archaeological museum is housed in the Convento da Nossa Senhora da Assunção, whose elegant 16th-century, two-storey cloister survived the earthquake of 1755. The ground floor's archaeological collection includes Roman and medieval funerary monuments, Manueline window frames, a Moorish stele inscribed with Arabic characters, and finds from the Roman villa at Milreu (► 36). Upstairs the miscellaneous collection includes everything from dress uniforms and heavy Sino-Portuguese rosewood furniture, to art nouveau vases and kitsch ashtrays.

✉ Largo Dom Afonso III ☎ 289 897400 ⏰ Oct–Mar Tue–Fri 9:30–5:30, Sat–Sun 11:30–5:30; Apr–Sep Tue–Fri 10–6, Sat–Sun 12–6 ♿ Few 💷 Moderate

MUSEU ARQUEOLÓGICO, LOULÉ

The Museu Municipal (Municipal Museum) and tourist office are built against the few remaining walls of the town's medieval castle. The museum displays flint tools and pottery fragments from the many prehistoric grave sites in the area, as well as a number of Iron-Age stele (incised grave markers).

✉ Rua de Paio Peres Correia 17 ☎ 289 415000 (ext. 211) ⏰ Mon–Fri 9–5:30, Sat 10–2 ♿ Few 💷 Free

MUSEU MARÍTIMO, FARO

Housed in the same building as the harbour authority, this museum contains model ships – from 15th-century caravels to modern naval gunships, as well as a collection of colourful shells and models explaining the techniques of the fishing industry. In contrast with today's high-tech factory ships, with sonar devices and sweep nets, the sardine and tuna boats shown here seem charmingly antiquated.

✉ Capitania do Porto de Faro ☎ 289 894990 🕔 Mon–Fri 2:30–4:30 ♿ Few 🎫 Moderate

MUSEU, MONCARAPACHO

This small town would be of little interest to visitors had not the local parish priest (who died in 1996) built up a remarkable small museum alongside the baroque Santo Cristo chapel (follow signs to 'Muscu'). It is filled with curiosities that offer a profile of the history and archaeology of the whole region: there are coins, stones from an old olive press, shackles once used to imprison African slaves, Napoleonic cannon balls, and clay scoops from Moorish-style water wheels. Among the Roman masonry are soldier's tombstones and a milestone that once stood alongside the main road from Faro to Seville. Upstairs, pride of place goes to a beautiful, 18th-century Neopolitan crib scene, with lively wood and porcelain figures of shepherds and kings. Beside the museum, the tiny 16th-century chapel is covered in 17th-century *azulejos*.

✉ 8km northeast of Olhão 🕔 Museu Mon–Fri 11–5 ♿ Few 🎫 Moderate 🍴 Cafés (€) around the main square 🚌 Buses from Olhão

Neolithic rocks on display in Silves's Museu Municipal de Arqueologia

MUSEU MUNICIPAL DE ARQUEOLOGIA, SILVES

The archaeological museum is built around the excavated remains of a Moorish house. The complexity and beauty of the well, with its stone flagged spiral staircase lit by arched windows, descending to the watery depths, makes you realise how impressive the Moorish city must have been. The museum explains the city's evolution from prehistory to recent times. The top floor leads out on to a restored section of the city wall, from where there is a view down over the old Moorish quarter.

✉ Rua das Porta de Loulé 14 ☎ 282 444832 🕔 Mon–Sat 9–6. Closed public hols ♿ Good 🎫 Moderate

MUSEU REGIONAL DO ALGARVE, FARO

The grainy pictures and displays of saddlery, straw-weaving, salt-panning, net-weaving and lace-making in this museum paint a picture of everyday life in the Algarve as it was until the mid-1970s, and still remains in the more remote rural regions. Among the fascinating exhibits are reconstructions of typical village interiors and displays of ornamented chimneypots.

✉ Praça da Liberdade ☎ 289 827610 🕔 Mon–Fri 9:30–12:30, 2:30–5:30. Closed Sat, Sun and public hols ♿ Few 🎫 Moderate

57

Children's Attractions

Zoomarine, Dolphin Show

THEME PARKS & WATER PARKS

The Algarve has four large water parks, and although half-day tickets are available you could easily spend a whole day at each. Facilities are graded so that children of all ages will find something to thrill and challenge them, from junior slides and pools for younger children to 'corkscrew slides' and 'black holes' for the older ones. Fully qualified lifeguards are on hand to ensure safety, and there are snack bars and restaurants for refuelling.

AQUASHOW, QUARTEIRA

Combined waterpark and bird garden with a wax museum.

✉ On the N396 just outside town ☎ 289 389396 🕐 Easter–Oct daily 10–6 (Jun–Aug till 7:30)

BIG ONE, ALCANTARILHA

Exciting attractions, with names like 'Raging Rapids', 'Flying Carpets' and 'Crazy Leap', make this a must for the daring. The park has the longest speed slide in the Algarve.

✉ On the N125 main highway at Alcantarilha ☎ 282 322827; www.bigone-waterpark.com 🕐 Daily 10–6. Closed Nov–Easter

KRAZY WORLD–ALGARVE ZOO, ALBUFEIRA

A real mixture of attractions from swimming pools to petting zoo to exotic animal show to a fairground.

✉ Signposted from the N125, Guia ☎ 282 574134 🕐 Sep–May daily 10–6; Jun–Aug 10–7:30

SLIDE AND SPLASH, ESTÔMBAR

Experience the exciting 'Black Hole' whirlpool here. Facilities include shops, bars and a restaurant. Slide and Splash runs buses in summer, collecting customers from pick-up points in the main coastal resorts.

✉ Just off the N125, at Vale de Deus, near Estômbar ☎ 282 341685 🕐 Daily 10–6. Closed Nov–Easter

ZOOMARINE, GUIA

One ticket provides entry to the marine zoo and water park. Shows featuring dolphins, seals and parrots are staged through the day, and other attractions include an aquarium, cinema, sea museum, funfair, swimming pools with slides and whirlpools, and restaurants.

✉ On the N125 at the Guia junction, near Albufeira ☎ 289 560300; www.zoomarine.com 🕐 Daily 10–6. Closed Nov–Easter

ATLANTIC PARK, QUARTEIRA

Thrilling slides for the energetic, with lots of long water slides and tunnels.

✉ On the N125 at Quatro Estradas, near Quarteira ☎ 289 397282 🕐 Daily 9–6. Closed Nov–Easter

TRAINS, BOAT TRIPS & JEEP SAFARIS

The Algarve railway travels from Vila Real de Santo António to Lagos through interesting coastal scenery. In Praia da Rocha, the Rocha Express road train runs along the promenade in summer, leaving Miradouro at half-hourly intervals from 10–12:30 and 3–6:30. Jeep safaris explore some of the lesser-known parts of the Algarve, travelling on unsurfaced roads.

MOUNT SAFARI, PRAIA DA ROCHA
✉ Rua Eng. José Bivar ☎ 282 420800

POLVO, VILAMOURA
Travel in high-speed rigid inflatable boats to catch sight of a dolphin.
✉ Marina de Vilamoura ☎ 289 301884 🕐 Trips daily

ZEBRA SAFARI, ALBUFEIRA
✉ The Strip ☎ 289 583300; www.zebrasafari.com

HORSE RIDING

The Algarve's numerous stables offer riding lessons for everyone from adults to infants and from beginners to seasoned hackers, usually with English-speaking instructors. Book by the hour or go trekking through glorious countryside or cantering along the beach on half- or full-day trips. Some stables will send transport to meet you and provide refreshments for longer rides.

TIFFANY'S RIDING CENTRE
✉ Lagos ☎ 282 697395

VALE NAVIO
✉ Albufeira ☎ 289 542870

MISCELLANEOUS

ALMANCIL KARTING, ALMANCIL
Karting track designed as a small replica of the Brazilian Grand Prix circuit, inaugurated by the late Ayrton Senna. Separate children's track.
✉ Sítio de Pereiras ☎ 289 399899; www.mundokarting.pt
🕐 Summer daily 9–8; winter daily 9–4

LAGOS ZOOLOGICAL PARK, BARÃO DE SÃO JOÃO
See various habitats that are home to exotic birds, monkeys, emus and wallabies, to name but a few. There are refreshment facilities and an area where children can interact with the animals.
✉ Sítio do Medronhal, Barão de São João ☎ 282 688236
🕐 May–Sep daily 10–7; Oct–Apr daily 10–5 💷 Expensive

OMEGA PARQUE JARDIM ZOOLÓGICO
Animal park dedicated to conservation and breeding of endangered species, including cheetah and rhino.
✉ On the N266 at Caldas de Monchique ☎ 282 911327
🕐 Apr–Sep daily 10–7; Oct–Mar 10–5:30

INDULGENCE

Fair-haired children may get fed up of being patted on the head or shoulders by strangers. But it is a fact of life that the Portuguese regard them as especially fortunate, so any would-be lottery-prize winner will want a bit of your child's luck. No harm is meant – the Portuguese love children. In restaurants, children are welcomed and indulged, and parents can bask in the extra attention that well-behaved families get wherever they go.

Playing in the sand at Praia De Faro

Places to Have Lunch

BURGAU BEACH BAR (€), BURGAU (▶ 62)

CAFÉ ALIANCA (€)
Forgive the slow service – the décor and ambience is the reason for being here, in the dimly lit interior of one of Portugal's oldest cafés.
✉ Praça Francisco Gomes 6, Faro ☎ 289 801621

FORTALEZA DA LUZ (€€), LUZ (▶ 63)

IMPERIAL (€€€), TAVIRA (▶ 69)

MURALHAS DE FARO (€€€), FARO (▶ 67)

A Cataplana dish

O SOEIRO (€), ALCOUTIM (▶ 68)

PARAÍSO DA MONTANHA (€), MONCHIQUE (▶ 65)

SÌTIO DO FORNO (€€), NEAR CARRAPATEIRA (▶ 62)
Fantastic high-level views along the cliffs of western Algarve, the vastness of the Atlantic Ocean and the freshest barbequed fish from the morning catch.

1692 (€€€), CALDAS DE MONCHIQUE (▶ 64)

SANTOLA RESTAURANT (€€), ARMAÇÃO DE PÊRA (▶ 64)

A restaurant in the Algarve

ALGARVE
where to...

Western Algarve

PRICES

Prices are approximate, based on a three-course meal for one without drinks and service:

€ = under €15
€€ = €15–€25
€€€ = over €25

OPENING HOURS

Most restaurants in the Algarve open from 10AM through to midnight, though smarter restaurants may close between 3 and 7, and some open only in the evening.

BARÃO DE SÃO JOÃO

CANGALHO (€€)

Rustic Portuguese cuisine is the speciality of this rural restaurant, located in a traditional farmhouse. The home-baked bread comes fresh from a wood-fired clay oven, as does the roast suckling pig, chicken *cabidela* and hunter's rabbit.

✉ Quinta Figueiras, Sítio do Medronho ☎ 282 687218 ⏰ Lunch, dinner. Closed Mon

BURGAU

ANCORA (€€)

Enjoy lovely sea views while you dine on delicious options from an adventurous menu: mussels cooked in Indian spices and pork in a fig sauce are among the imaginative offerings.

✉ Largo dos Pescadores ☎ 282 697102 ⏰ Dinner. Closed Mon in summer, Mon and Tue in winter

BEACH BAR (€)

Rock-bottom prices at this well-positioned beachside restaurant, with its seafront terrace, specialising in grilled fresh fish.

✉ Praia de Burgau ☎ 282 697553 ⏰ Lunch, dinner. Closed Mon

CASA GRANDE (€€)

Set in the former winery attached to a beautifully restored manor house, this restaurant serves Portuguese and vegetarian dishes. Reservations advised.

✉ On the Burgau to Praia da Luz road ☎ 282 697416 ⏰ Dinner. Closed Dec–Feb

THE PIG'S HEAD (€€)

The porcine theme at the Pig's Head is reflected in the décor of this English-style pub, and in the very popular pig roasts, served on Sundays. Portuguese, English and international dishes feature on the menu during the rest of the week.

✉ Luz road, east of Burgau ☎ 282 697315 ⏰ Lunch, dinner

CARRAPATEIRA

SÍTIO DO FORNO (€€)

Wonderful panoramic views of Amado beach from the terrace of this cliff-side restaurant, which specialises in barbecued fish caught in the family boat.

✉ Praia do Amado ☎ 963 558404 ⏰ Lunch, dinner. Closed Mon

O SÍTIO DO RIO (€€)

On the edge of Bordeira beach, this popular restaurant has a more varied menu than Sítio do Forno but the view isn't as spectacular.

✉ Praia Bordeira (on the coastal road) ☎ 282 973119 ⏰ Lunch, dinner. Closed Mon

LAGOS

A VACA (€€)

Swiss restaurant specialising in dishes of bockwurst, rosti and fillets of pork.

✉ 25–27 Rua Silva Lopes ☎ 282 764431 ⏰ Dinner. Closed Sun

DOM SEBASTIÃO (€€)

This popular restaurant, with its timbered ceiling, has an open-air terrace and an extensive menu.

✉ Rua 25 de Abril ☎ 282 762795 ⏰ Lunch, dinner. Closed Sun in winter

MILLENIUM JARDIN (€€)

An international menu with a range of fresh fish on ice. The restaurant is situated in an open terrace and mezzenine.

✉ 25 Rua 25 de Abril ☎ 282 762897 ⏰ Lunch, dinner

OS ARCOS (€€)

Os Arcos serves the very best in seafood and traditional Portuguese dishes. It has tables on the square and a large indoor dining room.

✉ Rua 25 Abril, 30 ☎ 282 763210 ⏰ Lunch, dinner. Closed Mon

PRAIA DA LUZ

FORTALEZA DA LUZ (€€)

The remains of the 16th-century fortress have been turned into a characterful restaurant. Fresh fish, Portuguese cuisine and flambé dishes, plus live jazz on Sundays.

✉ Rua da Igreja 3 ☎ 282 789926 ⏰ Lunch, dinner. Closed mid-Nov to mid-Dec

SAGRES

A TASCA (€€)

It's on the harbour in Sagres in a former market building, and specialises in fresh fish and shellfish.

✉ Sagres harbour ☎ 282 624177 ⏰ Lunch, dinner

BOSSA NOVA (€)

Pasta and pizzas, plus vegetarian dishes and seafood at this friendly restaurant.

✉ Avenida Comandante Matosa ☎ 282 624566 ⏰ Lunch, dinner

O TELHEIRA DO INFANTE (€€–€€€)

Good options of snack bar or full service restaurant (concentrating on seafood dishes) depending on your mood. Good sized terrace overlooking the beach.

✉ Praia de Mareta ☎ 282 624179 ⏰ Lunch, dinner

POUSADA DO INFANTE (€€)

Luxuriate in the comfortable ambience of this hotel restaurant serving locally caught fish, set on a cliff-top with sweeping views.

✉ Atalaia Point ☎ 282 624222 ⏰ Lunch, dinner

SALEMA

ATLÂNTICO (€€)

Smart modern restaurant just on the beachfront at Salema with a good-sized terrace. Excellent fresh fish but also meat dishes.

✉ Praia da Salema ☎ 282 695142 ⏰ Lunch, dinner

VILA DO BISPO

CAFÉ CORREIA (€)

Simple, rustic Portuguese restaurant that specialises in serving barnacles. Fish is the main offering on the extended menu; wine is from the cask.

✉ Rua 1 de Maio 4 ☎ 282 760985 ⏰ Lunch, dinner. Closed Sat

BARS AND *PASTELARIAS*

Bars are usually open all day, from early in the morning until late at night, serving coffee, soft drinks and alcohol. Most serve cheese, ham or *presunto* (cured ham) sandwiches, and there will usually be a small display of cakes. Just about every village, no matter how small, has a bar, so you are never very far from refreshment. The *pastelaria* is one step up: usually attached to a bakery, it serves a much more extensive range of cakes, as well as savoury snacks, such as quiche or salads, hot dogs and hamburgers. More often found in towns and cities than in villages, the *pastelaria* is where many city-dwelling Portuguese eat lunch, and most close at 7, as the smarter restaurants begin to open.

APPETISERS

When you eat in an Algarvian restaurant, the waiter will present you with a basket of delicious homemade bread, along with a selection of spreads – butter, cheese and sardine paste are the commonest – which many Portuguese will have instead of a starter. Some restaurants also serve home-cured olives and a range of nibbles – such as chopped vegetables dressed with garlic, herbs and oil – which make a delicious accompaniment to pre-dinner drinks.

63

Western Central Algarve

FISH ON THE MENU

Your favourite fish may not seem so familiar if the menu only has their names in Portuguese. Here is a short list of fish that you will frequently find on Algarvian menus: *atum* (tuna), *bacalhau* (salted cod), *cherne* (sea bass), *carapau* (mackerel), *pargo* (bream), *salmão* (salmon), *salmonete* (red mullet), *truta* (trout) and *espadarte* (swordfish).

ALGOZ

O JOÃO (€€)
Here you'll be surrounded by local people who come to enjoy hearty Portuguese specialities.
✉ Senhora do Pilar (on the same street as the Hermitage) ☎ 282 575332 🕐 Lunch, dinner

ALVOR

SOMEWHERE ELSE (€€)
Fun restaurant with Irish and Dutch owners. You cook your own meat or fish on heated lava stones.
✉ Rua Poeta João de Deus ☎ 282 458595 🕐 Lunch, dinner

ARMAÇÃO DE PÊRA

SANTOLA RESTAURANT (€€€)
Pretty restaurant next to the castle chapel, with a terrace overlooking the beach – great for a relaxed dinner. Fresh seafood is the speciality.
✉ Largo de Fortaleza ☎ 082 312332 🕐 Lunch, dinner

CALDAS DE MONCHIQUE

1692 (€€€)
A smart restaurant within the spa complex, with a beautiful formal dining room and sun-drenched terrace where you can enjoy a long lunch, romantic dinner or quick snack. International menu, with fine wines and cigars.
✉ Caldas de Monchique ☎ 282 910910 🕐 Lunch, dinner

CARVOEIRO

GRANDE MURALHA (€€)
This Sino-Portuguese restaurant has familiar and not-so-familiar dishes (curried squid and fried ice cream). For something down-to-earth, try the delicious sizzling prawns.
✉ Estrada do Farol, Praia do Carvoeiro ☎ 282 357380 🕐 Lunch, dinner

LE BISTROQUET (€€)
Small bistro-style French restaurant in the centre of town, with friendly service from the Dutch managers.
✉ Estrada do Farol, Praia do Carvoeiro ☎ 282 357743 🕐 Lunch, dinner. Closed Mon

TIA ILDA (€€)
With over 100 choices on the menu and 70 wines in stock there should be something for everyone; tapas, Italian choices and Portuguese specialities. Rooftop terrace.
✉ Rua do Monto Serrada ☎ 282 357380 🕐 Lunch, dinner. Closed Mon

FERRAGUDO

SUESTE (€€)
Fresh fish is a speciality of this restaurant, at the end of the fishing docks. Sit outside or eat in the dining room, with its 17th-century painted ceiling.
✉ Rua da Ribeira 91 ☎ 282 461945 🕐 Lunch, dinner. Closed Mon

MONCHIQUE

BICA-BOA (€€)
One of the Algarve's best restaurants, with regional and international dishes.

✉ Estrada de Lisboa ☎ 282 912271 ⏰ Lunch, dinner

PARAÍSO DA MONTANHA (€)

Popular for its excellent chicken *piri-piri*, and the mountain views.
✉ Estrada da Fóia ☎ 282 912150 ⏰ Lunch, dinner

QUINTA DE SÃO BENTO (€€€)

The views from this award-winning restaurant vie for attention with the grandeur of the building – the former summer residence of the royal House of Bragança – near the summit of Fóia. Specialises in game and also offers wild boar.
✉ Estrada da Fóia ☎ 282 912143 ⏰ Lunch, dinner

DONA BARCA (€)

One of Portimão's renowned fish restaurants, in a converted riverside warehouse. It serves fish straight off the boats and has live music in summer.
✉ Largo da Barca ☎ 282 484189 ⏰ Lunch, dinner

STEAKHOUSE DINAMARCA (€€)

For meat lovers in a town full of sardine and fish restaurants this Danish-owned restaurant serves prime Argentinian steaks and great apple pie.
✉ 14–16 Rua Santa Isabella ☎ 282 422072 ⏰ Lunch, dinner. Closed Mon

A PORTUGUESA (€)

This small, friendly restaurant in the heart of the tourist 'strip' concentrates on international cuisine with a few Portuguese specialities to tempt you.
✉ Avenida Tomás Cabreira ☎ 282 424175 ⏰ Lunch, dinner. Closed Sun (except Jul–Aug)

CASA DE ROCHA (€€)

Three terraces give stunning views of the coastline and this former summerhouse is a great place for a sunset meal. Traditional Portuguese dishes are served.
✉ Avenida Tomás Cabreira ☎ 282 419674 ⏰ Lunch, dinner

CAFÉ INGLÊS (€)

Opposite the cathedral and alongside the castle entrance, this café is housed in an elegant 1920s house originally built as the mayor's residence. Enjoy fresh-baked bread and cakes with tea, or more substantial snacks.
✉ Escadas do Castello 11 ☎ 282 442585 ⏰ Lunch, dinner. Closed Sat

CASA VELHA DE SILVES (€€)

Overshadowed by the gates to the old Moorish city, the Casa Velha offers traditional Portuguese grilled fish, *cataplana* (fish stew) and *espetada* (kebabs). The restaurant holds regular concerts of *fado* and other folk music.
✉ Rua 25 de Abril 13 ☎ 282 445491 ⏰ Lunch, dinner

ACCOMPANIMENTS

You do not normally need to order vegetables or salad separately with your main course. The dish will automatically be served with a selection of cooked seasonal vegetables, or a small salad of grated carrots and cabbage, with tomato and cucumber. Chips are the traditional accompaniment to meat dishes, and boiled potatoes are served with fish, unless you request otherwise.

Eastern Central Algarve

ALGARVIAN WINE

Local wines are inexpensive and quite strong – especially the reds, which are typically 13 or 13.5% alcohol. They are sold mostly as *vinho da casa* and, in traditional Portuguese restaurants, are drawn from a barrel. If you want a bottle of local wine, look for the Lagoa label. Wine experts tend to dismiss Algarvian wines, saying they lack subtlety. Softer and fuller flavoured wines come from the Alentejo, and are sold under the names of the co-operative producers, Borba, Redondo and Reguengos de Monsaraz.

ALBUFEIRA

LA TRAVESSA (€€)

Friendly service and good value is the signature of this cosy restaurant.
✉ Travessa dos Arcos 78
☎ 289 513299
🕐 Lunch, dinner

MUMTAZ (€€)

Considered one of the most authentic Indian restaurants along the coast. Balti and tandoori specialists (children's menu for kids who don't like spicy food).
✉ Avenida Sá Carneiro (Montechoro 'Strip') ☎ 289 542314 🕐 Dinner

O PENEDO (€€)

Delicious garlic clams are the speciality of this cliff-top restaurant.
✉ Rua Latino Coelho 15
☎ 289 587429 🕐 Lunch, dinner

ALMANCIL

CASA DE PORTUGUESA (€€)

One of the prettiest restaurants on the Algarve, with an interior of stucco and *azulejos*, the Casa de Portuguesa is family-friendly and serves excellent local cuisine.
✉ Vale Formosa (on the road to Areeiro) ☎ 289 393301
🕐 Lunch, dinner. Closed Mon

FUZIO'S (€€€)

A blend of Mediterranean and New World cuisine is offered in this beautifully renovated Portuguese house.
✉ Val do Lobo/Almancil Road
☎ 289 399019 🕐 Dinner. Closed Wed

SÃO GABRIEL (€€€)

One of a cluster of fine restaurants in the Almancil area, São Gabriel has earned a Michelin star. Reservations necessary.
✉ Lobo/Quinta do Lago
☎ 289 394521 🕐 Dinner. Closed Mon

LA PAELLA (€€)

If you have tried *arroz do marisco* (seafood rice), come here to find out how it compares with the Spanish favourite *paella*. The restaurant also serves a range of *tapas*.
✉ Estrada de Vale d'Aguas 26
☎ 289 393874
🕐 Lunch, dinner

ALTE

FONTE PEQUEÑA RESTAURANT/BAR (€)

Large restaurant with wood-panelled dining room and terraces overlooking the stream and springs. There is a wood fire in winter. The menu includes snacks and hearty meat dishes.
✉ Fonte Pequeña ☎ 289 478509 🕐 Lunch

FARO

ALIANÇA (€)

The food is unexciting and the service slow at this traditional café – one of the oldest in the country – but people come for the ambience of the dimly lit, wood-panelled 1920s interior.
✉ Praça Francisco Gomes 6
☎ 289 801621 🕐 Lunch

CIDADE VELHA (€€)

Atmospheric town-house restaurant in the old city

close to the cathedral and archaeological museum. Imaginative menu includes fresh clams steamed with coriander, dates wrapped in bacon, and prawns in beer.

✉ Rua Domingos Guieiro 19
☎ 289 827145
🕐 Lunch, dinner

MESA DOS MOUROS (€€€€)
A pretty converted house is home to this bijou restaurant with a small terrace. Inside, the small rooms are soothed by classical music.

✉ Largo da Sé 10
☎ 289 878873 🕐 Lunch, dinner. Closed Sun all day, Mon lunch

MURALHAS DE FARO (€€€)
This beautifully styled restaurant set in the old city walls serves Alentejo and Morrocan dishes. Lovely dining room and very pleasant terrace

✉ 1–7 Rue e Beco do Repuso
☎ 289 8248339
🕐 Lunch, dinner

LOULÉ

BICA VELHA (€€€)
Located in a characterful medieval building, claimed to be the oldest in Loulé, this excellent restaurant serves local fish with style. Popular, so book ahead.

✉ Rua Martim Moniz 17–19
☎ 289 463376 🕐 Dinner

O AVENIDA VELHA (€€)
This distinguished old restaurant is famous for its homemade bread, and small savoury dishes,

similar to Spanish *tapas*.

✉ Avenida José da Costa Mealha 40, first floor ☎ 289 462106 🕐 Lunch, dinner. Closed Sun

MUSEU DO LAGAR (€€)
A traditional Portuguese restaurant with dishes including wild boar, ostrich and buffalo. The huge vaulted interior gives a great atmosphere.

✉ Largo da Matriz 7 ☎ 289 416307 🕐 Lunch, dinner.

QUERENÇA

RESTAURANTE DE QUERENÇA (€€)
While away the siesta hours here, or enjoy a dinner with accordion music at weekends. Rabbit, wild boar, fish kebabs and lamb dishes. Book at weekends.

✉ Largo da Igreja ☎ 289 422540 🕐 Lunch, dinner. Closed Wed

VALE DO LOBO

LE CREPERIE (€)
The perfect place for a light lunch or snack, just off the beach at Val do Lobo. Salads, wraps, sandwiches, crepes and ice-creams.

✉ Vale do Lobo Praça
☎ 289 353429 🕐 Breakfast, lunch, dinner

MEMORIES OF CHINA (€€€)
One of a chain of smart Chinese restaurants. Faultless food, including the delicious sizzling three-seafood platter.

✉ David Lloyd Tennis Centre, Vale do Lobo ☎ 289 393939
🕐 Dinner. Closed Sat

DESSERTS

Two desserts that you will invariably find on the menu are *tarte* and *pudim*. Tarte can be made with many different ingredients, but nearly all have ground almonds as their base, mixed with flour and egg, poured into a pastry case and baked until golden. Some are additionally flavoured with lemon juice or honey syrup. *Pudim* is crème caramel, but not the individual servings you might expect in a French restaurant: Portuguese *pudim* is a substantial ring of steamed egg custard from which slices are cut to order. A more unusual choice, if you can find it, is *queijo de figo* – literally 'fig cheese' – made from layers of dried figs, ground almonds, cinnamon and chocolate.

Eastern Algarve

REGIONAL VARIATIONS

In coastal regions, grilled fresh fish predominates, and regular deliveries to even the most distant inland village means that it is also a major element on their menus, though not in such great variety. Inland you are more likely to find lamb, kid, pork and chicken, while restaurants in the Barrocal mountains will often have a section of the menu devoted to game: wild boar, quail, partridge, hare and rabbit in particular. Perhaps the most distinctive cuisine is that of the Guadiana River valley, where the river itself is the source of the eels, lampreys and mullet that are typical of local restaurants.

ALCOUTIM

O SOEIRO (€)

In a shady corner beside the parish church, O Soeiro is often frequented by local ferrymen waiting for passengers crossing to Spain. Terrace tables have river views. Watch your chicken or pork grilling over a charcoal brazier. ✉ Rua do Município 4 ☎ 281 546241 🕐 Lunch. Closed Sat and Sun

TI AFONSO (€)

Very good and busy restaurant serving Portuguese meat dishes. No river view, but the food and atmosphere make up for that. ✉ Praça da República ☎ 967 292169 🕐 Lunch, dinner. Closed Mon

BARRANCO DO VELHO

A TIA BIA (€€)

This fine restaurant is popular with walkers and cyclists who come to enjoy the rare landscape of the forested Serra do Caldeirão mountains. Specialising in game dishes, the restaurant often has wild boar on the menu, as well as partridge with cabbage, and pumpkin with rabbit. ✉ Barranco do Velho crossroads ☎ 289 846425 🕐 Lunch, dinner

MONTE GORDO

O CRUZEIRO (€€)

A choice location and appetising menu make this excellent for a leisurely meal. ✉ Praia de Monte Gordo ☎ 281 542288 🕐 Lunch, dinner. Closed Wed

DOURADO (€€)

One of a few timber shacks on the beach, with shaded terraces. Serves *cataplana* (fish stew) and a Portuguese dishes. ✉ Avenida Infante Dom Henrique ☎ 281 512202 🕐 Lunch, dinner

OLHÃO

O BOTE (€€)

Across the street from the market, O Bote serves delicious grilled meat and fish. Small terrace but large indoor dining area. ✉ Avenida 5 de Outubro ☎ 289 721183 🕐 Lunch, dinner. Closed Sun

SANTA BÁRBARA DE NEXE

LA RÉSERVE (€€€)

Much-lauded restaurant. Mainly French food is served stylishly, but at a high price. Reservations are essential in summer. ✉ Estrada de Esteval ☎ 289 999234 🕐 Lunch, dinner. Closed Tue

SÃO BRÁS DE ALPORTEL

LUÍS DOS FRANGOS (€)

Locals flock here for the barbecued chicken, chips, salad and local wine. ✉ Tavira road ☎ 289 842635 🕐 Lunch, dinner

POUSADA DE SÃO BRÁS (€€)

Elegant restaurant in state-run hotel with beautiful views over the hills. Try *caldeirada de borrego* (lamb stew).

✉ São Brás de Alportel ☎ 289 843205 🕐 Lunch, dinner

TAVIRA

BEIRA RIO (€€)

This elegant riverside restaurant has a range of vegetarian dishes and is noted for its garlic-flavoured quail. Book ahead in summer.

✉ Rua Borda d'Água da Assêca 46–52 ☎ 281 323165 🕐 Lunch, dinner. Closed last three weeks in Nov and Jan–Easter

CASA COTA (€)

Dine on the roof terrace for views over the characterful rooftops of Tavira. Specialises in charcoal-grilled meats.

✉ Rua João Vaz Corte Real 38 ☎ 281 324873 🕐 Lunch, dinner

IMPERIAL (€€€)

Grand restaurant renowned for chicken and rice dishes, and its *serrabucho de marisco* (seafood with pork).

✉ Rua José Pires Padinha 22 ☎ 281 322306 🕐 Lunch, dinner

O CANTINHO DAS ESPETADAS (€€)

Traditional Portuguese restaurant with regional specialities that also hosts *fado* on Saturday nights.

✉ 22 Rua Dr Augusto da Silva Carvalho ☎ 918 801292 🕐 Dinner. Closed Sun

O PÁTIO (€€)

Try lobster or tiger prawns flambé, or the more modestly priced clams *cataplana*, couscous or fish kebab.

✉ Rua António Cabreira 30 ☎ 281 323008 🕐 Lunch, dinner

PRAÇA VELHA (€€)

Good choice for lunch while sightseeing with a small air-conditioned dining room or plenty of seating outside to watch the world go by. Mixture of Portuguese and international dishes.

✉ Rua José Pires (in the Mercado da Riviera) ☎ 281 325866 🕐 Lunch, dinner

QUATRO ÁGUAS (€€)

It's a short step from the boat to the table for the seafood at this atmospheric restaurant, alongside the fish warehouse.

✉ Quatro Águas ☎ 281 325329 🕐 Lunch, dinner

VILA REAL DE SANTO ANTÓNIO

CAVES DO GUADIANA (€€)

On the river bank, this restaurant specialises in Portuguese seafood and spicy African-style cod.

✉ Avenida da República 89 ☎ 281 544498 🕐 Lunch, dinner. Closed Thu dinner

O CORAÇÃO DE CIDADE (€€)

Large and popular, with tables spilling on to the pavement. The vast menu includes English sandwiches, Spanish *tapas*, Andalucian *gazpacho* and squid *Sevilhana*, pizzas and chicken *piri-piri*.

✉ Rua Cândido dos Reis ☎ 081 512972 🕐 Lunch, dinner

LIQUEURS

Algarvians have a gift for turning their local fruits into alcoholic liqueurs. The most popular drink with which to end the meal is *medronho*, a potent spirit distilled from the strawberry-coloured fruits of the arbutus tree, which grows in profusion in the Monchique region. Lovers of almonds will adore the delicious sweet liqueur called *amêndoa amarga*, also sold as *Algarviana*. Another good choice is *brandymel*, a warming blend of brandy and honey.

Western Algarve

PRICES

Prices are for a double room, including breakfast and tax:
€ = under €90
€€ = €90–€150
€€€ = over €150

OPENING

Unless otherwise indicated, all hotels are open year-round.

HOTELS

Many seafront hotels in the Algarve are of a very high standard, with luxurious accommodation in well-maintained gardens, overlooking glorious beaches. They are also quite expensive, though often cheaper if booked as part of a package holiday. Conversely, tour companies often charge more for the cheaper hotels than if you book direct. Prices drop dramatically in winter and many four- and five-star hotels offer very good value, often matching the rates of much lower-class hotels. Nearly all hotels in the Algarve include breakfast as part of the room price. Half- and full-board terms are also available at the more expensive hotels.

BURGAU

CASA GRANDE (€)

This characterful guest house is packed with antiques and collectibles. Artists and writers love its faded grandeur and so will anyone searching for something different from a modern hotel.
✉ 8650 Burgau ☎ 282 697416; www.nexus-pt.com/casagrande

LAGOS

CAZA DE SÃO GONÇALO (€)

Atmospheric old town house in the centre of town where the rooms are decorated in typical Portuguese style with period furniture. Garden and terrace.
✉ Rua Cândido dos Reis ☎ 282 762171

PRAIA DA LUZ

BELAVISTA (€€)

The Belavista sits above the sheltered beach at Praia da Luz, with its rooms grouped amphitheatre-style around the swimming pool. The rooms are spacious and comfortable and there is plenty to do here, from scuba diving and dancing for the teenagers, to yoga and meditation classes.
✉ Beach road ☎ 282 788655; www.belavistadaluz.com

HOTEL LUZ BAY (€€€)

Mexican 'pueblo style' hotel opened in 2003, set around an atrium with a great pool area. Other facilities include tennis and squash courts, a sauna and Turkish bath. The tastefully decorated rooms are equipped with satellite TV, mini fridge and safe. Only a couple of minutes walk from the excellent sandy beach. Good rates in winter.
✉ Rua du Jardim, Praia da Luz, 8600 Lagos ☎ 282 789640

SAGRES

PENÃO D HENRIQUE (€)

Simple but a good budget hotel located in central Sagres with balconies overlooking Mareta beach. Within strolling distance to a range of cafés and restaurants.
✉ Praça da República ☎ 282 60003

POUSADA DO INFANTE (€€)

Located on the cliff-tops, this splendid *pousada* is built in traditional Algarvian style, with red-tiled roofs, ornate chimneys and a cloister-like loggia providing shaded terraces to its rooms. Facilities include a swimming pool and tennis courts, and there is fishing and watersports in Sagres.
✉ 8650 Sagres ☎ 282 624222; www.pousadas.pt

SALEMA

ESTALAGEM INFANTE DO MAR (€€€)

A new resort in spacious grounds between Budens and the resort of Salema. There is a range of sports and leisure facilities. A good location for exploring Western Algarve.
✉ Praia da Salema, 8650–193, Budens ☎ 282 690100

Western Central Algarve

ALVOR

PESTANA DELFIM HOTEL (€€€)
In lush grounds above the Três Irmãos beach; golf and sports near by.
✉ Praia Três Irmãos, 8501–904
☎ 282 400800;
www.pestana.com

ARMAÇÃO DE PÊRA

VILA VITA PARC (€€€)
Distinguished hotel with Moorish-inspired domes and shady cloisters. Facilities include pools, a playground, tennis and squash courts, a pitch-and-putt golf course, health club, five restaurants and a nightclub.
✉ Apartado 196, P-8365 Armação de Pêra ☎ 282 315310; www.vilavita.com

CALDOS DE MONCHIQUE

COMPLEXO TERMAS MONCHIQUE (€–€€)
A range of accommodation at the thermal spa from a four-star inn, three-star pension and self-catering apartments.
✉ Caldos de Monchique
☎ 282 910910;
www.monchiquetermas. com

CARVOEIRO

TIVOLI ALMANSOR (€€€)
Well placed for a number of golf courses, and on the cliff-tops above its own cove sheltered by sandstone cliffs. Facilities include a pool and shops.
✉ Praia Vale Covo, Carvoeiro, 8400 Lagoa ☎ 282 351100;
www.tivolihotels.com

FERRAGUDO

CASABELA HOTEL (€€€)
Luxurious hotel in a picturesque setting above the Praia Grande beach; an excellent base for walking and watersports. Heated outdoor pool, tennis courts and restaurant.
✉ Vale da Areia, Ferragudo, near Portimão ☎ 282 461580

PORTIMÃO

LE MERIDIEN PENINA (€€€)
The perfect family resort hotel, with supervised activities for children in July and August, including excursions, competitions, tennis, golf, mountain biking and horse riding. There's plenty for parents as well, including golf and watersports.
✉ Apartado 146, Montes de Alvor, 8502 Portimão ☎ 282 415415; www.lemeridien-hotels.com

PRAIA DA ROCHA

HOTEL ORIENTAL (€€€)
Beautifully designed luxury hotel with distinctive oriental touches overlooking the beach at Praia da Rocha.
✉ Avenida Tomás Cabreira
☎ 282 480800; www.tdhotels.pt

SILVES

HOTEL COLINA DOS MOUROS (€)
Modern hotel in Moorish style, across the river with wonderful views of the town. Facilities include gardens, a pool, children's pool, bar and restaurant.
✉ 8301 Silves ☎ 282 440420

SELF-CATERING

Most accommodation in the Algarve is in self-catering villas and apartments, often set in a complex around pleasant gardens, with central facilities such as a bar, swimming pool, shop and restaurant. Villas usually have a small kitchen with fridge and gas cooker, a garage and small garden, a living room with TV and simply furnished bedrooms with en suite bathrooms. A maid will clean the villa and change the linen once a week. Advance booking is essential for the main holiday period. (Travel agents' brochures are full of offers, but you can often get a higher standard of accommodation, and better prices, by renting privately.)

Eastern Central & Eastern Algarve

HIGH AND LOW SEASON PRICES

Hotel prices reflect the demand at different times of year. January and February are the cheapest, and many retired people take advantage of the very low rents on self-catering villas to escape the cold weather of northern Europe. Christmas, Easter and school half-term weeks are popular, but not greatly expensive – at these times of year the availability of flights to the Algarve is more a limiting factor than rental prices, so make arrangements well in advance. Spring comes relatively early, from late February and through March, and is one of the best times of year to visit for weather, temperature and wildlife July and August are the hottest and by far the most expensive months.

ALBUFEIRA

HOTEL BALTUM (€€)
No frills hotel 50m from the famed town beach and 50m from the town bars and restaurants. The perfect budget location for sunbathing and partying.
✉ 26 Avenida 25 de Abril
☎ 289 589102;
www.hotelbaltum.com

QUINTA DA BALAIA (€€€)
Resort hotel set in lush grounds, offering luxurious one- to five-bedroom villas. Close to the golf course, with sporting facilities on site.
✉ Branqueira, Praia Santa Eulália, 8200-594 ☎ 289 586575

SHERATON ALGARVE (€€€)
Awarded Portugal's coveted Silver Medal for excellence in tourism services, the Sheraton Algarve, also known as Pinecliffs, is a complete resort, with a 9-hole golf course and golf academy and a large outdoor pool and tennis-courts. Guests have access to miles of sandy beaches. Wind-surfing, pedalos, Jet skis and waterski facilities are all available, and there is a choice of both casual and more formal restaurants.
✉ Praia da Falésia, 8200 Albufeira ☎ 289 500100;
www.pinecliffs.com

ALMANCIL

QUINTA DO LAGO (€€€)
In a magnificent setting on the Ria Formosa estuary, each room has its own garden terrace and there are tennis courts, pools, a gym, sauna, solarium and masseuse, and two golf courses. The hotel hires bicycles and arranges fishing trips and most watersports.
✉ 8135 Almancil
☎ 289 396666;
www.quintadolagohotel.com

ALTE

ALTE HOTEL (€€)
Many who come here are walkers, taking advantage of Alte's central location to explore the fascinating Barrocal countryside, with its limestone caves, cliffs and valleys and unspoiled Portuguese way of life. Rooms are simple but comfortable. Facilities include tennis courts and a pool, plus a restaurant specialising in fresh fish, game and rural dishes, such as pigs' trotters.
✉ Montino, Alte, 8100 Loulé
☎ 289 478523

LOULÉ

LOULÉ JARDIM HOTEL (€)
This recently renovated early 20th-century town mansion makes an excellent inland base. Rooms are simply furnished but the roof terrace has a pool and bar (summer only).
✉ Praça Manuel de Arriaga
☎ 289 413094

MONTE GORDO

HOTEL NAVEGADORES (€€)
One of the largest hotels in Monte Gordo just 100m

from the superb beach. The hotel is 1970s in style and rooms are simple, but there is an indoor pool, gym and a spa on site.

✉ Rua Gonçalo Velho, 8900
☎ 281 510860

SÃO BRÁS DE ALPORTEL

POUSADA SÃO BRÁS (€€)

In the peaceful foothills of São Brás de Alportel, this state-run hotel, one Portugal's *pousada* chain, was built in 1944 but has been modernised. The rooms are decorated in Algarvian style, and the facilities include a pool and tennis court.

✉ 8150 São Brás de Alportel
☎ 01 848 9078;
www.pousadas.pt

TAVIRA

VILA GALÉ ALBACORA (€€€)

Beautiful low-level hacienda-style hotel located on the river 3km outside Tavira. An excellent place to relax, with pools, spa and gym, and from where to tour the eastern Algarve.

✉ Quatro Águas ☎ 281 380800; www.vilgale.pt

VALE DO LOBO

LE MERIDIEN DONA FILIPA (€€€)

Part of the manicured and prestigious Vale do Lobo estate, the Dona Filipa this relatively small, elegant hotel enjoys a privileged position beside the sea, a few feet from the beach and surrounded

by golf courses. Guests enjoy discounted green fees and an early start at the São Lourenço Club, rated one of Europe's best. There are three floodlit tennis courts and a heated outdoor swimming pool. The two restaurants have excellent wine lists.

✉ Vale do Lobo, 8136 Almancil
☎ 289 394141;
www.lemeridien-hotels.com

VILAMOURA

TIVOLI MARINOTEL (€€€)

This is a large hotel overlooking the marina. The resort lies right on your doorstep, and there is a beach near by. Rooms are luxurious, and include a computer with Internet access. The hotel offers a range of sports on site.

✉ 8125-901 Vilamoura
☎ 289 389988;
www.tivolimarinotel.com

VILA REAL DE SANTO ANTÓNIO

HOTEL GUADIANA (€)

This grand, historic hotel is classed as a national monument. Its interior includes frescoed walls, elegant marble statues and delightfully decorated rooms. Some rooms look across the River Guadiana to Spain. The ferry to Ayamonte leaves from the opposite side of the road. Seville and Granada are within driving distance and the long, sandy beaches of Monte Gordo are only 5 minutes away.

✉ Avenida da República 94, Vila Real de Santo António, 8900 Monte Gordo ☎ 281 511482

GRADINGS AND PRICES

Hotels in the Algarve are graded from 1 to 5 stars, but there is considerable variation between the cost of a 3-star hotel on the coast, for example, and one in a less tourist-visited inland town – prices drop rapidly once you move away from the coast. For rock-bottom prices, look out for the simple *pensão* or residential guest houses, often in town centres, offering clean, no-frills accommodation. Above this, a 3-star hotel will probably consist of a modern, purpose-built block, with clean and comfortable rooms and en suite bathrooms, a restaurant and small pool. Buildings with greater character may style themselves as an *estalagem* or *albergeria*, and anything styled as a *quinta* is probably a luxurious converted manor house, at the centre of its own expansive estate.

Antiques, Artesanato & Artists

SHOP OPENING HOURS

Shops in the Algarve are generally open from Monday to Friday 9–1 and 3–7, and on Saturday 9–1. During the summer, many stay open through the siesta period, especially those in tourist resorts, and until 10pm at night, or later. Supermarkets in resorts open on Sundays and holidays. During the winter, opening hours are less predictable. Some shops catering exclusively for tourists close altogether from the beginning of November through to Easter.

ANTIQUES

LAGOS

CASA DO PAPAGAIO

You can't miss this shop because of its live parrot, outside the door. Inside, the cramped store is packed with everything from junk to genuine antique statuary.
✉ Rua 25 de Abril ⏰ Mon–Fri 10–1, 3–7, Sat 10–1

PORTIMÃO

A TRALHA

A vast warehouse of objects large and small. Also shops in Almancil and Albufeira.
✉ Largo de Digue
⏰ Mon–Sat 10–1, 3–7

VILAMOURA

SECULO XIX

Interesting shop with cut glass, jewellery and china.
✉ Marina Plaza ⏰ Summer 10–8; winter 10–1, 3–8

ARTESANATO

Artesanato shops specialise in typical Portuguese products. These include dolls made from hessian, woven baskets, cork products, lace tablecloths, woollen shawls and chunky sweaters, handmade rugs, brightly painted earthenware jars, painted cockerels and models of traditional sailing vessels, caravels, carved in wood.

ALBUFEIRA

O PIPOTE

Tiny shop selling quality ceramics, basketry and embroidery.
✉ Rua Joaquim Manuel Gouveia 15 ⏰ Summer daily 10–8; winter Mon–Sat 10–1, 3–8

PAU DE PITA

Range of *artesanato* but concentrates on traditional Portuguese pottery.
✉ Rua 5 de Outubro
⏰ Summer Sun–Mon 9–8; winter Mon–Sat 9–1, 3–7

ALTE

CAFÉ REGIONAL

Café that doubles as a shop for hand-painted plates and basketry.
✉ Just south of the parish church, in Alte's main square
⏰ Mon–Sun 8–1, 3–7

GALERIAS IVETTE

Painted plates and realistic silk flowers are among the best buys.
✉ Just southeast of the parish church, in Alte's main square
⏰ Mon–Sun 8–1, 3–7

CABANAS

O VALE

A shop and café selling garden pots and local products.
✉ Almargem, on the N125 north of Cabanas ⏰ Daily 9–8

CARVOEIRO

A PRAÇA VELHA

Excellent range of pottery and *artesanato*.
✉ Rua dos Pescdores
⏰ Mon–Sun 9–6 (later in summer)

FARO

PORTA DA MOURA

A range of ceramics, textiles and toys.

✉ Rua do Repouso 5
🕐 Mon–Sun 10–8

LAGOS

POTICHO
Ceramics, basketwork and embroidery.
✉ Rua 25 de Abril 24 🕐 Daily 9–7. Closed Sun in winter

LOULÉ

CENTRO DE ARTESANATO
Perhaps the best display of *artesanato* in the Algarve. Unusual items include ornaments made from palm leaves and wood caravels.
✉ Rua da Barbacã
🕐 Mon–Sun 8–1, 3–7

O ARCO
Hand-painted plates.
✉ Rua das Almadas
🕐 Mon–Sun 8–1, 3–7

MONCHIQUE

CASA DOS ARCOS
Specialises in folding wooden chairs and tables but also has good knitwear and rugs.
✉ Rua Calouste Gulbenkian
🕐 Mon–Sun 9–7. Closed 12:30–3 and Sun in winter

QUERENÇA

AFARROBINHA
Barn-like shop for loal food and handicrafts.
✉ Largo Igreja 🕐 Mon–Fri 10–1, 3–6, Sat 10–1

SAGRES

ARTESANATO ALGARVIO
Fine *azulejos*, and other local products. On the main road into Sagres.
✉ N268 🕐 9–8

TAVIRA

ALART
Modern pottery and crafts.
✉ Rua de Caleria 🕐 Mon–Fri 10–1, 3–7, Sat 10–1

PORTAS DO CASTELO
Good range of modern cork products, plus other quality *artesanato*.
✉ 1–3 Praça da República
🕐 Summer Mon–Sun 9–7; winter Mon–Sat 9–1, 3–6

VILA REAL DE SANTO ANTÓNIO

ESTABELECIMENTOS SOL DOURADO
Huge product range.
✉ Rua Dr Teófilo Braga
🕐 Mon–Fri 10–1, 3–8, Sat 10–1

ARTISTS

SAGRES

VIRGILIO COSTA
This Portuguese artist brings his personal style to the Algarve landscapes he paints.
✉ Shop: on the main road into Sagres from Vila do Bispo; Studio: Rua Dr Fransisco, Quinta do Borel, Amadora 🕐 Apr–Sep 10–12, 3–6

SILVES

ESTUDIO DESTRA
Ceramic artist Kate Swift produces and fine range of *azulejos* in modern styles and undertakes commissions.
✉ Largo Jeronimo Osorio
🕐 Summer Sun–Mon 10–7; winter Mon–Sat 10–12, 2–6

THE COCKEREL OF BARCELOS
Souvenir shops throughout Portugal sell cockerels of all sizes, in many different colours and guises, and the Algarve is no exception. This national symbol stands for honesty and truthfulness. According to a popular folk story, the guest at a banquet in Barcelos (Northern Portugal) was publicly accused of theft. Hauled before a judge, he was pronounced guilty and sentenced to hang. To prove his innocence, the condemned man pointed to a cockerel that was being served to the judge on a silver platter and declared that the bird would crow. To everyone's astonishment the bird stood up and duly crowed.

Basketry, Ceramics & Pottery

BASKETRY

Baskets make lightweight and inexpensive presents. Made all over the Algarve, and sold in *artesanato* shops, the capacious bags are derived from the sort that peasant farmers have developed over the centuries for carrying produce to and from the fields and markets – flexible shoulder bags and panniers made from straw or *esparto* grass.

BASKETRY

TAVIRA

ARTESANATO REGIONAL BAZAR TANGER
Basket weavers can sometimes be seen at work here making a range of products.
✉ Rua José Pires Padinha
🕐 Mon–Sat 10–1, 3–7. Closed Sun

CERAMICS & POTTERY

ALBUFEIRA

GALERIA LABISA
A range of modern styles of china, glass and pewter.
✉ 16 Avenida da Liberdade
🕐 Summer Mon–Sun 10–8; winter Mon–Sat 10–7

ALTE

CERAMICA D'ALTE
Interesting ceramics are produced on site.
✉ Estrada National 124
🕐 10–1, 3–6

LAGOS

O CAIXOTE
Traditional pottery from all over Portugal is sold here, including replica chimneypots, mugs and painted plates and the ubiquitous pottery rooster.
✉ Rua 25 de Abril 🕐 Mon–Sat 8–1, 3–7

LOULÉ

ALEGRETE
Terracotta jars, garden ornaments and pots with an attractive patina.

✉ Rua Miguel Bombarda 66–68
🕐 Mon–Sun 8–1, 3–7

CASA LOUART
Pretty hand-painted pottery, with bold designs of fruit and flowers.
✉ Rua Dom Paio Peres 19
☎ 289 413794 🕐 Mon–Sun 8–1, 3–7

MONCHIQUE

O MOINHO
Variety of traditional styles of pottery and *azulejos*.
✉ Barracão (main road between Monchique and Portimão)
🕐 Sun–Mon 9–7

MONTE GORDO

CASA CARAVELA
Pottery, cookware and linens – traditional and modern.
✉ Avenida Infante D Henrique
🕐 Summer Mon–Sun 9–7. Closed Sun winter

PORCHES

OLARIA ALGARVE POTTERY
Patterned ceramics. Watch the artists at work.
✉ N125, Porches 🕐 10–6

PORTIMÃO

CASA CELIARTE
Bright, hand-painted ceramics.
✉ Rua 5 de Outubro 🕐 10–1, 3–6

PRAIA DA ROCHA

CERÂMICA
This tiny converted fisherman's cottage is filled with ceramics.
✉ Avenida Tomas Cabreira
🕐 Mon–Sun 9–6

Clothing & Leatherware

CLOTHING

ALBUFEIRA

ADRIANA
Stocks the latest styles in women's summer clothing and accessories.
📧 30 Largo Duarte
🕐 Mon–Sun 9–7 (till 10 in summer)

FARO

ANTÓNIO ZUCANNEL
Designer fashions for women: Versace, Polo and many more big names.
📧 Rua de Santo António 48
🕐 Mon–Fri 10–1, 3–7, Sat 10–1

PALLORAM
Come to Palloram for the best in upmarket men's fashions.
B Rua de Santo António 53 D
Mon–Fri 10–1, 3–7, Sat 10–1

LEATHERWARE

Portuguese craftsmanship in leather is renowned throughout Europe. The Algarve has a number of shops selling beautifully made items at good-value prices. Algarvian leather workers also specialise in tooled leather, and there has been a long tradition of saddle-making in the region.

ALBUFEIRA

KITANDA
All sorts of quality leather goods, including bags, purses, gloves and jackets are sold at Kitanda.
📧 Rua Alves Correia
🕐 9–1, 2–6 (till 8 in summer)

FARO

OBERON
Smart shoes, handbags and a range of accessories.
📧 Rua de Santo António 67
🕐 Mon–Sun 10–8

LAGOS

CRISBEL
A comprehensive range of leather handbags, suitcases and purses.
📧 Rua 25 de Abril 62
🕐 Mon–Fri 9–1, 2–6, Sat 9–1

SIROCCO
Sirocco is on Rua Cândido dos Reis, one of the main shopping streets in Lagos, which is known for leather boutiques. The shop focuses on African crafts, including leather lamps and mirrors from Morocco.
📧 Rua Cândido dos Reis 37

LOULÉ

MALAS VINHAS
The leather goods on sale here include sandals, boots and handbags.
📧 Rua 5 de Outubro 55
🕐 Mon–Sat 8–1, 3–7. Closed Sun

PORTIMÃO

CHIC SHOES
Specialises in handmade leather boots and shoes.
📧 Rua Direita 🕐 Mon–Sat 10–1, 3–8

LEATHER FACTORY
The Leather Factory sells everything from shoes and belts to waistcoats and skirts – take your pick.
📧 Rua Dr J V Mealha
🕐 Mon–Sat 10–1, 3–8

ALGARVIAN POTTERY

Ceramic techniques were introduced to the Algarve by the Moors and the tradition has never died. Among the region's products are terracotta pots for use in the garden, and hand-painted jugs, plates and bowls, decorated with brightly coloured fruit and flower motifs. Also popular are hand-painted cockerels (*gallos*) in every size and shape, and miniature versions of the ornate Algarvian chimneys that are seen on older houses throughout the region. In addition, *azulejos* are still made – thick, chunky irregular tiles with blue and white or polychrome painted decorations. Genuine antique *azulejos* are sold singly and are expensive, but modern tiles are sold in sets for use as floor or wall decorations.

Markets

LOULÉ'S MARKET

If you want the best combination of permanent market and street market, go to Loulé on a Saturday. Head for the Moorish-style building in Avenida José da Costa Mealha. Here, every street in the vicinity of the covered market has its smallholders, from farmers with sacks of grain and animal feed to souvenir stalls piled with painted cockerels and plates. For gourmets, there is a delightful range of home-produced food on sale, including herb-marinated olives, dried figs, almond-based sweets, bundles of dried spices, sweet cheeses, hams and spicy sausages.

PERMANENT MARKETS

Every town of any size has a permanent covered market, which opens every day except Sunday from 6:30AM and which stays open until around 1PM. There are usually separate areas for fish and for fruit and vegetables, and some have butcher's shops in separate premises around the perimeter of the hall. Larger markets also have stalls selling home-baked bread, mountain-cured ham and local sheep's-milk cheeses. Farmers sometimes set up stalls in the streets around the market entrance, selling anything from a rabbit or a chicken to bunches of herbs or jars of honey. You may also find clothes and bric-á-brac. Four of the best produce markets are:

Lagos
The market is in the renovated old market building on Rua das Portes de Portugal.
✉ Rua Vasco de Gama
🕓 Mon–Sat 8–1

Loulé
Set in a striking, tiled, Moorish-style building, dating from the 1930s, and with the most varied range of stalls of any market in the Algarve.
✉ Praça da República
🕓 Mon–Sat 8–1

Olhão
The biggest and best in the region – two adjacent halls built in Moorish style, with fish and shellfish for sale in one and fruit and vegetables in the other.
✉ Avenida 5 de Outubro
🕓 Mon–Sat 8–1

Silves
Everything under one roof, including bread from a wood-fired oven.
✉ Rua J Estevão 🕓 Mon–Sat 8–1

STREET MARKETS

Itinerant merchants travel from town to town setting up stalls at what are sometimes called 'gypsy markets' or 'country markets'. In addition, some towns have a 'Saturday market', which centres around the covered market, but attracts many additional stallholders in the surrounding streets. The stalls selleverything you could ever want.

MAIN MARKETS:

Albufeira: 1st and 3rd Tuesday of the month (in Orada to the west of the town).
Almancil: 1st and 4th Sunday of the month.
Alvor: 2nd Tuesday of the month.
Lagos: 1st Saturday of the month.
Quarteira: every Wednesday.
Loulé: every Saturday.
Monchique: 2nd Friday of the month.
Portimão: 1st Monday of the month (next to the station).
Sagres: 1st Friday of the month (opposite the post office).
Silves: 3rd Monday of the month.

Shopping Malls & Miscellaneous

SHOPPING MALLS

ALBUFEIRA

ALGARVESHOPPING
The largest and most modern shopping centre along the coast, with 133 shops and a nine-screen cinema complex.
✉ On the N125, west of Albufeira 🕐 10AM–11PM

FARO

FORUM ALGARVE
This new mall has won prizes for its open-air design. Over 130 shops and a fast-food court make it a popular haunt for the population of the capital.
✉ On the N125, Sitio des Figuras 🕐 10–8

QUINTA DO LAGO

QUINTA SHOPPING
A stylish low-rise mall of 63 shops, restaurants and beauty salons, around a central plaza.
✉ Quinta do Lago ☎ 289 398247 🕐 10–8

MISCELLANEOUS

ALBUFEIRA

GARRAFIERA SOARES
A good selection of Portuguese wine, spirits and port to stock your drinks cabinet back home.
✉ Largo Duarte 🕐 Mon–Sun 9–10

7 MARES
A range of imported oriental objects, jewellery and shells.
✉ Rua 5 de Outubro 🕐 Summer Mon–Sun 10–9; winter Mon–Sat 10–1, 3–7

ALMANCIL

FLORIDA GOLF
Everything for the golf fanatic: shoes, bags, accessories, books, gifts.
✉ Vale de Éguas, N125 🕐 Mon–Sat 8–1, 3–7

GRIFFIN BOOKSHOP
The Algarve's best-stocked English-language bookshop. Good range of fiction and non-fiction for children and adults, plus second-hand books.
✉ Rua 5 de Outubro 206-A ☎ 289 393904 🕐 Mon–Sat 8–1, 3–7

PANDA GALERIA DE ARTE
Stocks and sources a range of modern art by established and up and coming artists.
✉ Barros de Almancil, Escanxinas 🕐 Mon–Sat 10–1, 3–7

LAGOS

TRIARTE
Designer jewellery, blown glass and hand-painted silk. Also makes goods to order.
✉ Rua da Vedoria 🕐 9–7

MONTE GORDO

GEMAS DO MUNDO
Crystals, semi-precious stones and fossils from around the world.
✉ Rua Gil Eanes 29a 🕐 9–8

OLHÃO

A MARGERIDA
Soft furnishings and picture frames.
✉ Rua do Comércio 🕐 Mon–Fri 10–1, 3–7, Sat 10–1

WINES AND SPIRITS
Just head for any supermarket in the Algarve to find a comprehensive stock of local products. Most local wines are best drunk in the Algarve, but one or two travel well: look for the names Arade or Lagoa on the label.
You might also like to buy classic Portuguese wines from beyond the Algarve, such as Dão, *vinho verde* or port. Local liqueurs include distilled arbutus berries (*medronho*) and *amêndoa amarga*, a delicious almond-based liqueur.

Nightlife

CASINOS

Casinos offer free entry to slot machines and video games. Proof of age must be provided to gain entry to the gaming machines, and there may be a charge. Visitors must be smartly dressed. Some casinos offer a nightly dinner and floorshow.

Monte Gordo
✉ Avenida Marginal
☎ 281 530800

Praia da Rocha
✉ Hotel Casino Algarve
☎ 282 400200

Vilamoura
✉ Praia da Marina
☎ 289 310000

FILM FESTIVAL

Film buffs may be interested in the Algarve's International Film Festival in May, when Portuguese and foreign films are shown at cinemas in Alvor, Lagoa, Lagos and Loulé, in their original language; ☎ 01 851 3615 for further details.

FADO

Fado is unique to Portugal; it is claimed to have its origins in African slave music, but the music developed its present form in mid-19th-century Lisbon. *Fado* means 'fate', and each 3-minute song expresses the sadness and yearning occasioned by lost or unrequited love, or the vicissitudes of life. Two musicians accompany: one plays the pear-shaped *quitarra portuguesa* (a 12-stringed Portuguese guitar), while the other plays the bass line on a Spanish guitar.

ALBUFEIRA

HOTEL SOL E MAR
✉ Rua José Bernadino de Sousa
☎ 282 500800 ⓘ *Fado* performances Fri 10PM

ALMANCIL

QUINTA DO LAGO
✉ Hotel Quinta do Lago, Quinta do Lago ☎ 289 350350
ⓘ *Fado* peformances Thu

RESTAURANTE LISBOA ANTIGA
✉ 85 Avenida 5 Outubro
☎ 289 391883 ⓘ *Fado* performances Thu 8PM

CARVOEIRO

RESTAURANTE FERNANDO'S STONE STEAK
✉ Monte Carvoeiro ☎ 282 358690 ⓘ *Fado* performances Fri 8PM

QUARTEIRA

RESTAURANTE DALLAS
✉ Avenida Francisco Sá Carneiro
☎ 289 313293 ⓘ *Fado* performances Sat 8PM

SILVES

QUINTA POMONA
✉ 26-r/c 5 Outubro ☎ 282 416350 ⓘ *Fado* performances Wed, Fri 8PM

TAVIRA

RESTAURANTE O CANTINHO DES ESPETADAS
✉ 22 Rua Dr Augusto de Silva Carvalho ☎ 918 801292
ⓘ *Fado* performances Sat 7PM

VILAMOURA

HOTEL VILA GALÉ AMPALIUS
✉ Avenida da Praia ☎ 289 303900 ⓘ *Fado* performances Mon 9PM

CINEMAS

Many of the Algarve's multi-screen cinemas are in shopping complexes. Films are shown in their original language, usually English.

ALBUFEIRA

ALGARVE SHOPPING
✉ On the N125, west of Albufeira ☎ 289 560350

FARO

FORUM ALGARVE
✉ On the N125, Sitio das Figuras ☎ 289 865249

PORTIMÃO

MODELO DE PORTIMÃO (SHOPPING CENTRE)
✉ Quinta da Malata, Lote 1
☎ 282 415272

Boat Trips, Fishing & Watersports

BOAT TRIPS & FISHING

LAGOS

BOM DIA
Travel along the coast in a tall-masted sailing ship and use smaller boats to explore marine grottoes.
✉ Lagos marina
☎ 282 764670

LAGOS KAYAK CENTRE
Guided freshwater kayak trips along the river.
✉ Motel Âncora, Estrada do Porto do Mós ☎ 282 782718; www.blue-ocean-divers.de

PORTIMÃO

BLUE MARLIN
Fishing trips for shark, marlin and swordfish.
✉ Portimão Marina
☎ 282 425866

PIRATE SHIP ADVENTURE CRUISE
Cave exploration, sailing or beach BBQ can be enjoyed from this fully rigged caravel sailing ship.
✉ Rua Vasco do Gama
☎ 967 023840

SAGRES

COASTAL TOURS
Explore the awe-inspiring cliffs of Fim do Mundo and the windswept Costa Vicentina. Also 3-hour fishing trips.
✉ Turinfo, Praça de Republica
☎ 282 620003 ⊙ Tue & Thu (half days), Sat (full day)

VILAMOURA

POLVO
Company with several boats offering luxury motor yatchs and dolphin-spotting trips to small boat charter.
✉ Vilamoura Marina ☎ 289 301884

RIVER CRUISES

MONTE GORDO

RIVER GUADIANA CRUISE
✉ Rua Tristao vaz Teixeira
☎ 281 510201

PORTIMÃO

ARADE RIVER CRUISE
✉ Leãozinho Arade River Cruises, Portimão harbour
☎ 282 415156

WATERSPORTS

CARVOEIRO

DIVERS COVE PORTUGAL
Training, certification and accompanied dives.
✉ Quinta do Paraíso, Praia de Carvoeiro ☎ 282 356594; www.diverscove.de

LAGOS

BLUE OCEAN DIVERS
Trips for qualified divers, equipment hire and training to advanced level.
✉ Motel Âncora, Estrada do Porto do Mós ☎ 282 782718; www.blue-ocean-divers.de

SILVES

SLIVES WATERSKI CENTRE
Jet ski, kneeboarding, rings, banana and boat charters on a freshwater reservoir.
✉ Barragem de Silves
☎ 964 465614

HELICOPTER FLIGHTS

If you would rather have a bird's-eye view of the coastline, splash out on a sightseeing helicopter flight. Contact Sky Zone at the Aerodrome Municipal de Portimão, Montes de Alvor, 8500-059, Alvor ☎ 282 459926; www.skyzone.pt

Keeping Fit

CYCLE HIRE

Hiring a bicycle is a great way to explore the Algarve. Many local councils in the region have created cycle lanes and marked routes along the coast and through the countryside. Bicycles can be rented from:

Algarve2Bike
✉ Largo do Mercado, Albufeira ☎ 289 585886

Sport Nautica
✉ Rua Jacques Pessoa 26, Tavira ☎ 281 324371

Vilar du Golfe
✉ Quinta do Lago ☎ 289 352000

OUTDOOR PURSUITS

MONCHIQUE

ALTERNATIVTOUR MONCHIQUE

Guided hiking, rappelling, cycle tours and mountain bike tours in the Algarve hinterland.
☎ 282 420804

SPAS & BEAUTY TREATMENTS

Many of the Algarve's top hotels now have magnificent spas where you can cleanse and relax. Estética have a wide range of treatments and have salons in the following locations:
Barringtons
✉ Val do Lobo ☎ 289 398775
Four Seasons Country Club
✉ Quinta do Lobo
☎ 289 357154
Sheraton Algarve
✉ Albufeira ☎ 289 501331
Pestana Hotel
✉ Alvor ☎ 282 400935

SPORTS FACILITIES

PRAIA DA LUZ

The facilities at the Luz Bay and Ocean clubs are open to non-residents and include swimming pools, saunas, a Turkish bath, gym, mini-golf, tennis and squash courts.
✉ Avenida Pescadores, Praia da Luz, 8600 Lagos ☎ 282 789472

VALE DO LOBO

BARRINGTONS

Apart from the well-known golf academy, with its floodlit driving range and instruction, this complex includes squash courts, a cricket pitch with nets, a fitness centre, sauna, Turkish bath and Jacuzzi, indoor and outdoor swimming pools and a snooker room.
✉ Vale do Lobo ☎ 289 351940; www.barringtons-pt.com

VILAMOURA

VILAMOURA TENNIS CENTRE

Just off the resort's marina, the tennis club has 12 courts. Equipment hire and individual or group tuition is available.
✉ Vilamoura ☎ 289 310169

WALKING TOURS

For gentle exercise of body and mind, some local councils organise walking tours of their major towns. Here is a selection:
Albufeira
Tours of the medieval town centre and the Archaeological Museum.
✉ Cultural department of the Town Council, Rua Centenario Velha ☎ 289 588957
Aljezur
Tours of the historic centre.
✉ Town Council, Rua do Republica ☎ 282 998102
Faro
Tours of the Algarvian capital's historic centre.
✉ The Archaeology Museum, Largo Dom Afonso III
☎ 289 897400
Tavira
Choose from three different tour routes, each starting at the tourist office, on Rua da Galeria.
✉ Tavira Development Agency, Rua da Liberdade
☎ 281 321946

Golf

The Algarve is a popular destination for golfing holidays. Large numbers of visitors come here for no other reason than to spend a week perfecting their skills. The region has 29 courses, and some of them are renowned throughout the world for their challenging terrain and beautiful surroundings.

The following courses are among those highly rated by golfers:

ALVOR

ALTO GOLF

This cliff-top course enjoys superb views of the sea and the Serra de Monchique mountains. Designed by Sir Henry Cotton, the challenging course is famous for its 16th hole, one of the longest in Europe. There is also a golf school with practice bunker and putting green. 18 holes, par 72.

✉ Quinta do Alto do Poço, Alvor
☎ 282 460870

CARVOEIRO

PESTANA GOLF

The base for the David Leadbetter Golf Academy, with two 18-hole courses.
✉ Carvoeiro ☎ 282 340900

VALE DE MILHO

Nine-hole, par-27 course, with water hazards.
✉ Apartado 273, Carvoeiro
☎ 282 358502

VALE DA PINTA

New 18-hole course, built around an old olive grove.
✉ Carvoeiro ☎ 282 340900

VALE DO LOBO

PINHEIROS ALTOS

This par-72, 18-hole course begins in attractive pine woods, while the back nine holes run alongside the Ria Formosa Nature Reserve.
✉ Quinta do Lago ☎ 289 359910

QUINTA DO LAGO

Designed by Henry Cotton, the two 18-hole, par-72 courses feature lakes and challenging bunkers. The Portuguese Open and other international tournaments are regularly hosted here.
✉ Quinta do Lago
☎ 289 390700

SAN LORENZO

To play this 27-hole course (with three 9-hole loops) you must be a guest at the Dona Filipa (► 73) or Penina hotels. Keen golfers consider the expense worthwhile for the chance to play this highly rated golf course, with its famous 7th hole (on the yellow loop) straddling two ravines.
✉ Quinta do Lago
☎ 289 396522

VILAMOURA

The Vilamoura estate, west of Faro, has four courses designed for a range of abilities, from the testing Vilamoura I to the 27-hole Vilamoura III with three 9-hole combinations, among lakes.
✉ Vilamoura ☎ Old Course 289 310341; Pinhal 289 310390; Laguna 289 310180; Millennium 289 31088

REMEMBER

Almost all golf courses in the Algarve require a handicap certificate and most have a dress code. Remember to check your tee-off time when booking.

ALGARVE
practical matters

WHAT YOU NEED

	Some countries require a passport to remain valid for a minimum period (usually at least six months) beyond the date of entry — contact their consulate or embassy or your travel agent for details.	UK	Germany	USA	Netherlands	Spain
● Required ○ Suggested ▲ Not required						
Passport/National Identity Card		●	●	●	●	●
Visa (regulations can change — check before booking your journey)		▲	▲	▲	▲	▲
Onward or Return Ticket		○	○	○	○	○
Health Inoculations		▲	▲	▲	▲	▲
Health Documentation (➤ 90, Health)		○	○	○	○	○
Travel Insurance		○	○	○	○	○
Driving Licence (National)		●	●	●	●	●
Car Insurance Certificate (if own car)		●	●	●	●	●
Car Registration Document (if own car)		●	●	●	●	●

WHEN TO GO

Faro

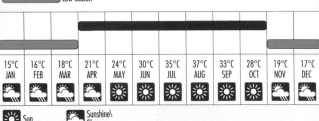

High season

Low season

15°C JAN	16°C FEB	18°C MAR	21°C APR	24°C MAY	30°C JUN	35°C JUL	37°C AUG	33°C SEP	28°C OCT	19°C NOV	17°C DEC

 Sun   Sunshine\Showers

TIME DIFFERENCES

GMT 12 noon	Portugal 12 noon	→ Germany 1PM	← USA (NY) 7AM	→ Netherlands 1PM	→ Spain 1PM

TOURIST OFFICES

In the UK
Portuguese National Tourist Office
22–25A Sackville Street
London W1X 1DE
☎ 09063 640610
Fax: 0207 494 1868
www.rtalgarve.pt

In the USA
Portuguese National Tourist Office
590 Fifth Avenue, 4th Floor
New York
NY 10036
☎ 212/354 4403
Fax: 212/764 6137;
www.portugal.org

ARRIVING

It is possible to drive to the Algarve from all parts of continental Europe, but most visitors arrive by air. Faro airport (☎ 289 800800) is served by scheduled and charter flights from most European airports. Because of the region's popularity as a winter destination, seats on direct flights get booked up well in advance and you might have to fly via Lisbon and drive. TAP Air Portugal is the national airline (in Faro ☎ 289 800200; www.tap.pt)

Faro Airport
Kilometres to city centre

Journey times

🚌 N/A

🚆 15 minutes

🚗 10 minutes

4 kilometres

MONEY

The euro (€) is the official currency of Portugal. Euro banknotes and coins were introduced in January 2002. Banknotes are in denominations of 5, 10, 20, 50, 100, 200 and 500 euros; coins are in denominations of 1, 2, 5, 10, 20 and 50 cents, and 1 and 2 euros.

Euro traveller's cheques are widely accepted, as are major credit cards, although cash can be more useful in the countryside. Credit and debit cards can also be used for withdrawing euro notes from automatic teller machines (ATMs). Banks can be found in most towns, although they do not necessarily offer the best deal for changing money when charges are taken into account.

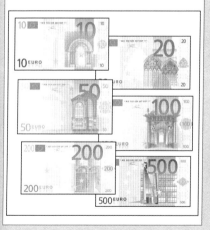

TIME

The Algarve observes Greenwich Mean Time during the winter months; during the summer, from late March to late October, the time is GMT plus one hour.

CUSTOMS

YES

From another EU country for personal use (guidelines):
800 cigarettes, 200 cigars,
1 kilogram of tobacco
10 litres of spirits (over 22%)
20 litres of aperitifs
90 litres of wine, of which 60 litres can be sparkling wine
110 litres of beer

From a non-EU country for your personal use, the allowances are:
200 cigarettes OR 50 cigars OR
20 grams of tobacco
1 litre of spirits (over 22%)
2 litres of intermediary products (e.g. sherry) and sparkling wine
2 litres of still wine
50 grams of perfume
0.25 litres of eau de toilette
The value limit for goods is 175 euros.

Travellers under 17 years of age are not entitled to the tobacco and alcohol allowances

NO

Drugs, firearms, ammunition, offensive weapons, obscene material, unlicensed animals.

EMBASSIES AND CONSULATES

UK
☎ 282 490750

Germany
☎ 289 803148

USA
☎ 21 727 3300
(Lisbon)

Netherlands
☎ 289 820903

Spain
☎ 281 544688

87

TOURIST OFFICES

Algarve Tourism Regional Office

● Avenida 5 de Outubro 18
8000 Faro
☎ 289 800400
Fax: 289 800489

Local Offices

● Albufeira
Rua 5 de Outubro 18
☎ 289 585279

● Faro
Rua da Misericórdia 8–11
☎ 289 803604

● Lagos
Rua Vasco da Gama, São João
☎ 282 763031

● Loulé
Edifício do Castelo
☎ 289 463900

● Monchique
Largo dos Chorões
☎ 282 911189

● Monte Gordo
Avenida Marginal
☎ 281 544495

● Olhão
Largo Sebastião M Mestre
☎ 289 713936

● Portimão
Avenida Zeca Afonso
☎ 282 416556

● Silves
Rua 25 de Abril
☎ 282 442255

● Tavira
Rua da Galeria 9
☎ 281 322511

NATIONAL HOLIDAYS

J	F	M	A	M	J	J	A	S	O	N	D
1	(2)	(2)	1(2)	1	1(1)		1		1	1	4

1 Jan	New Year
Feb (dates vary)	Shrove Tuesday and Ash Wednesday
Mar/Apr	Good Friday
Mar/Apr	Easter Monday
25 Apr	Day of the Revolution
1 May	Labour Day
Jun (dates vary)	Corpus Christi
10 Jun	National Day
15 Aug	Feast of the Assumption
5 Oct	Republic Day
1 Nov	All Saints' Day
1 Dec	Restoration of Independence Day
8 Dec	Feast of the Immaculate Conception
25 Dec	Christmas Day
26 Dec	St Stephen's Day

OPENING HOURS

○ Shops	● Main Post Offices
● Offices	● Museums/Monuments
● Banks	● Pharmacies

8AM	9AM	10AM	NOON	1PM	2PM	4PM	5PM	7PM

□ Day   □ Midday

□ Evening

Shops catering to tourists open all day in the high season, until 9 or 10 in the evening, including Sundays and public holidays.
Larger stores and supermarkets increasingly ignore the lunch break and are open continuously from 9 to 7, with some supermarkets staying open until 10 (until 5 on Sundays).
Pharmacies open late on a duty rota (posted on pharmacy doors). Times of museum and church opening vary greatly – see individual museums for details.

ELECTRICITY

The power supply in Portugal is: 220 volts AC.

Sockets take two-pronged continental plugs, so an adaptor is needed for non-continental applances, and a transformer for devices operating on 100–120 volts.

TIPS/GRATUITIES

Yes ✓ No ✗		
Restaurants (service included)	✓	10%
Bar service	✓	small change
Taxis	✓	10%
Tour guides	✗	
Porters	✓	€1
Chambermaids	✗	
Hairdressers	✓	10%
Cloakroom attendants	✓	small change
Toilets	✗	

PUBLIC TRANSPORT

Trains
Railway line follows the south coast from Lagos in the west to Vila Real de Santo António in the east. Recent upgrades (2002-04) to the track all along the 130km line ensure a smoother service but being single-track, journey times can be longer than distances suggest. Stations can be 6km or more from the towns that they serve, so check the map before deciding to use the train. It is cheap, however, and provides views of some fine coastal scenery. Tourist offices have timetables, and tickets should be bought before you get on the train, or else you risk a fine.

Buses
Modern express bus services link most towns in the Algarve. Services are provided by a number of companies. EVA is the biggest, and it sells a useful Passe Turístico (Tourist Pass), which allows unlimited use of the network for three or seven days. Bus routes principally follow the main roads, and so are not a reliable way of exploring the more remote countryside. Timetables and route maps are available from tourist offices and main bus stations *(terminal rodoviário)*. Have plenty of small change ready when boarding.

Ferries
Although most people now travel from Portugal to Spain along the motorway bridge that links the two countries across the Guadiana, ferries do still operate. The car and passenger ferry from Vila Real to Ayamonte departs at 40-minute intervals throughout the day, and fishermen ferry passengers from Alcoutim to San Lúcar on demand. Ferry services also take visitors to the barrier islands in the Ria Formosa Nature Reserve during the summer months, departing from Tavira and Olhão at regular intervals during the day.

CAR RENTAL

The major car rental firms are represented in the Algarve, as well as several local companies that offer slightly cheaper rates. All rental firms send a courtesy bus to meet you at the airport on arrival, transporting you to their depot on the Faro airport road; alternatively, they will deliver the car to your hotel or villa.

TAXIS

In towns, it is usual to hire taxis from a rank. They may stop if flagged down, especially in the countryside. Rates for some journeys are fixed. Short journeys across town should be metered. For longer journeys, you can negotiate an hourly rate. Try to find a driver who speaks your language and who has a modern well-maintained car.

CONCESSIONS

Students/Youths: Museums have lower rates of admission for students, and entry is free for children. Bring a passport or student card as proof of your age.

Senior Citizens: Many senior citizens come to the Algarve for the winter months, attracted by warm weather, a low cost of living and heavily discounted low-season long-stay rates. Ask travel agents specialising in Portugal for details.

DRIVING

Speed limit on motorways (autoestradas): **120kph; minimum: 40kph**

Speed limit on main roads: **90kph**

Speed limit on urban roads: **60 or 40kph**

Seat belts must be worn in front seats at all times and rear seats where fitted.

Random breath-testing. Never drive under the influence of alcohol.

Petrol *(gasolina)* comes in two grades: lead-free *(sem chumbo)* and 4-star *(super)*. Diesel *(gasóleo)* is also available. Most villages and towns have a petrol station, and they are generally open from 8 to 8.

All the car rental companies in the Algarve run their own breakdown and rescue services, details of which will be given to you when you rent your car. Main highways have orange SOS telephones for use in an emergency. Members of motoring organisations such as the AA and RAC can use the services of the ACP (Automóvel Clube de Portugal) ☎ 213 180100; www.acp.pt

Random roadside police checks can impose heavy fines on motorists who are not carrying proof of insurance, rental documents, driving licence and passport.

PHOTOGRAPHY

What to photograph: the Algarve's wild coastline, wind-eroded sandstone cliffs, markets, flowers, traditional costumes, donkey carts and ploughs drawn by horse or mule.
Best time to photograph: the light is best before 10AM; after this the intensity of the sun can bleach out details. Sunsets can be spectacular in the west.
Buying film: most hotels have shops selling film and batteries, and there is usually at least one specialist photo shop in every town, selling film and offering processing services.

PERSONAL SAFETY

Theft from cars and other petty crime is increasingly a problem. If you are the victim of theft, get help from a hotel or holiday representative because they know the correct procedures and can deal with the bureaucracy. To make an insurance claim you must report thefts to the local police station and get a copy of the written statement.

- Leave your valuables in the hotel safe.
- Don't leave valuables in cars.
- Don't leave unattended valuables on the beach or poolside.
- Beware of pickpockets.

National Police assistance:
☎ **112**
from any call box

TELEPHONES

Telephones booths can be found in every town and are plentiful in the resorts. On rare occasions where a booth cannot be found the local bar usually has a public phone. Most phones only take phone cards or credit cards. Phone cards (for 50, 120 or more units) are sold at newsagents and cafés. A 50-unit card will give you around 5mins of international calling time. To call the Algarve from the UK, dial 00 351 (the international country code for Portugal) then the 9-digit number which starts with a 3-digit area code (282, 289 or 281).

International Dialling Codes	**(From the Algarve to:)**		
UK:	00 44	Germany:	00 49
USA & Canada:	00 1	Netherlands:	00 31
Spain:	00 34		

POST

Post offices *(correios)* are found in main towns. In Faro, the most central post office is on Largo do Carmo, and post restante services are available here, and at all main post offices. Stamps can be bought from newsagents and hotel kiosks. Open: main office Mon–Fri 8:30 or 9–6, Sat 9–12:30. Smaller offices close 12:30–2:30.

HEALTH

Insurance
Nationals of EU member countries can get medical treatment in state hospitals with the relevant documentation (Form E111 for UK nationals), although private medical insurance is still advised and is essential for all other visitors. Most private clinics and doctors in the Algarve will treat you in your hotel provided you have insurance cover.

Dental Services
Dental services in the Algarve are excellent. Dentists advertise their services in the free English and German-language magazines available from most hotels, and in monthly publications such as *Algarve Living*.

Sun Advice
The sun can be intense in the Algarve at any time of the year, and it is possible to burn with less than an hour's exposure. If you are out walking on cliff-tops or bare hills, it is best to cover vulnerable parts of your body, including your neck, legs and arms.

Drugs
Chemists *(farmácia)* are open Mon–Fri 9–1 and 3–7, and Sat 9–1. Some open through lunch, and there is a late-night duty rota, posted in pharmacy windows. Take supplies of any drugs that you take regularly, since there is no guarantee that they will be available locally. However, many drugs are available from chemists in Portugal that require prescriptions in other countries. This is partly because pharmacists are skilled paramedics, trained to diagnose a range of problems and sell appropriate medicines.

Safe Water
Tap water is safe to drink, but can be unpleasant to taste because of the minerals it contains. Bottled water is widely available; ask for fizzy water *(água com gás)* or still *(água sem gás)*.

LANGUAGE

The language of the Algarve is Portuguese, but most hoteliers, shopkeepers and restaurateurs also speak English and German. Portuguese is easy to understand in its written form if you already know a Romance language – such as French, Italian or Spanish. When pronounced, however, it could easily be mistaken for a Slavic language. Two sounds are distinctive to Portuguese: vowels accented with a tilda sound like **owoo** (so bread, **pão**, is pronounced **powoo**) and the s and z, which are pronounced **zsh** (so **notas**, banknotes, is pronounced **notazsh**).

hotel	hotel/estalagem	a double room	quarto de casal
do you have a room?	tem um quarto livre?	a twin room	quarto com duas camas
I have a reservation	tenho um quarto reservado	with bathroom	com banho
		one night	um noite
how much per night?	qual e o preço por noite?	key	chave
		sea view	vista a mar
a single room	um quarto simples	gents/ladies	senhores/senhors

bank	banco	can you change?	pode trocar?
exchange	office câmbios	pounds/dollars	libras/dólares
post office	correio	do you take?	aceitam?
coins	moedas	credit card	cartão de crédito
banknotes	notas	traveller's cheque	cheque de viagem
receipt	recibo	cheque	cheque
the change	troco	how much?	quanto custa?

breakfast	pequeno almoço	beer	cerveja
lunch	almoço	menu	lista
dinner	jantar	red wine	vinho tinto
table	uma mesa	white wine	vinho branco
starter	entrada	water	água
main course	prato principal	tea	chá
dessert	sobremesa	coffee (black)	um bica
bill	conta	coffee (white)	café con leite

airport	aeroporto	which way to?	como se vai para?
bus	autocarro	how far?	a que distância?
bus station	estação de autocarro	where is?	onde está
bus stop	paragem	car	carro
a ticket to	um bilhete para	petrol	gasolina
single	ida	petrol station	posta de gasolina
return	ida e volta		

yes	sim	good evening/night	boa noite
no	não	excuse me	desculpe
please	por favor	you're welcome	está bem
thank you (male)	obrigado	not at all	de nada
thank you (female)	obrigada	how are you?	como está?
hello	olá	well, thank you	bem, obrigado (a)
goodbye	adeus	do you speak English?	fala inglês?
good morning	bom dia	I don't understand	não compreendo
good afternoon	bom tarde		

REMEMBER

● Faro airport is small and does not have expansive shopping facilities.

● You must report to the departure terminal of the airport no later than the check-in time indicated on your ticket.

● You must comply with the import regulations of the country you are travelling to (check before departure).

Index

TwinPack
Algarve

Written by Christopher Catling
Contributions from Lindsay Bennett
Editorial management by Apostrophe S Limited

A CIP catalogue record for this book is available from the British Library.

ISBN-10: 0 7495 4333 7
ISBN-13: 978 0 7495 4333 4

Material in this book may have appeared in other AA publications.

Published by AA Publishing, a trading name of Automobile Association Developments Limited, whose registered office is Southwood East, Apollo Rise, Farnborough, Hampshire, GU14 0JW. Registered number 1878835.

© **AUTOMOBILE ASSOCIATION DEVELOPMENTS LIMITED 2005**
First published 2005

Colour separation by Keenes, Andover.
Printed and bound by Times Publishing Limited, Malaysia

ACKNOWLEDGEMENTS
The pictures in this book are from the Automobile Association's own library (AA WORLD TRAVEL LIBRARY) and were taken by CAROLINE JONES, with the exception of the following:
M BIRKITT 23b, 36, 42b, 47b; MICHELLE CHAPLOW Front Cover (fisherman, church), 5b, 14, 16, 17, 18, 20b, 21t, 26t, 26b, 28t, 28b, 29t, 29b, 30b, 31t, 31b, 32t, 32b, 33t, 33b, 37b, 39, 40t, 40c, 43, 45b, 54b, 57, 90l; J EDMANSON Front Cover (pottery), 27t, 27b, 30t, 45t, 50b, 61t; ALEX KOUPRIANOFF Front Cover (fruit), 15, 19, 21c, 37t, 44b, 48, 52t, 85t; ANNA MOCKFORD and NICK BONETTI Back Cover cb; PETER WILSON 23t

A01922
Cover maps produced from mapping © Mairs Geographischer Verlag/Falk Verlag, 73751 Ostfildero, Germany
Fold out map © Mairs Geographischer Verlag/Falk Verlag, 73751 Ostfildero, Germany

TITLES IN THE TWINPACK SERIES
• Algarve • Corfu • Costa Blanca • Costa del Sol • Cyprus • Gran Canaria •
• Lanzarote & Fuerteventura • Madeira • Mallorca • Malta & Gozo • Menorca • Tenerife •

Dear **TwinPack** Traveller

**Your comments, opinions and recommendations are very important to us.
So please help us to improve our travel guides by taking a few
minutes to complete this simple questionnaire.**

*You do not need a stamp (unless posted outside the UK). If you do not want to cut this page from your
guide, then photocopy it or write your answers on a plain sheet of paper.*

Send to: **The Editor, AA TwinPack Travel Guides,
FREEPOST SCE 4598, Basingstoke RG21 4GY.**

Your recommendations…

We always encourage readers' recommendations for restaurants, nightlife or shopping – if
your recommendation is used in the next edition of the guide, we will send you a ***FREE***
AA TwinPack Guide of your choice. Please state below the establishment name,
location and your reasons for recommending it.

_____

_____

_____

_____

Please send me **AA TwinPack**
    Algarve ❏ Corfu ❏ Costa Blanca ❏ Costa del Sol ❏ Cyprus ❏
    Gran Canaria ❏ Lanzarote & Fuerteventura ❏ Madeira ❏
    Mallorca ❏ Malta & Gozo ❏ Menorca ❏ Tenerife ❏
    (*please tick as appropriate*)

About this guide…

Which title did you buy?
    AA *TwinPack* _____
Where did you buy it? _____
When? m m / y y

Why did you choose an AA *TwinPack* Guide? _____

_____

_____

_____

_____

Did this guide meet your expectations?
    Exceeded ❏ Met all ❏ Met most ❏ Fell below ❏
    Please give your reasons _____

_____

_____

continued on next page…

Were there any aspects of this guide that you particularly liked? _____

_____

_____

Is there anything we could have done better? _____

_____

_____

About you...

Name (*Mr/Mrs/Ms*) _____

Address _____

_____

_____ Postcode _____

Daytime tel no _____

Please only give us your mobile phone number if you wish to hear from us about other
products and services from the AA and partners by text or mms.

Which age group are you in?

Under 25 ☐ 25–34 ☐ 35–44 ☐ 45–54 ☐ 55–64 ☐ 65+ ☐

How many trips do you make a year?

Less than one ☐ One ☐ Two ☐ Three or more ☐

Are you an AA member? Yes ☐ No ☐

About your trip...

When did you book? m m / y y   When did you travel? m m / y y

How long did you stay? _____

Was it for business or leisure? _____

Did you buy any other travel guides for your trip?

If yes, which ones? _____

Thank you for taking the time to complete this questionnaire. Please send it to us as soon as
possible, and remember, you do not need a stamp (*unless posted outside the UK*).

Happy Holidays!